MW01204935

# His Third,
# Her Second

# His Third, Her Second

*a novel*

## PAUL ESTAVER

The author wishes to acknowledge the generous assistance
of the National Endowment for the Arts.

Published in the
United States of America by

Soho Press, Inc.
One Union Square
New York, NY 10003

Library of Congress Cataloging-in-Publication Data

Estaver, Paul.
His third, her second : a novel / by Paul Estaver.
p.       cm.
ISBN 0-939149-25-7
I. Title.
PS3555.S74H57    1989
813'.54—dc19       88-33680
CIP

Book design and composition by The Sarabande Press

Manufactured in the United States of America
First Edition

*to Lynn*

# PART

# I

# 1

## 1. Henry

Henry had always wanted children. When the years passed without them, he talked Edith into adopting a little girl. All they knew about Libby was that she had been plucked out of a foster home at twenty-one months. She came with the clothes on her back and a stuffed animal worn beyond recognition. She arrived asleep and woke terrified.

It took a day for them to realize it was Henry she was scared of. This child screamed at the approach of the man who'd waited so long to adopt her. And she clambered after Edith like a bear cub—after Edith, who was repelled by babies, who could barely stand to touch her. Before the placement the welfare people had hardly talked to Edith, they were so relieved to find a home for a foundling.

Libby was beautiful—black-eyed and black haired. Her skin was as luminous as a pond in June at daybreak. That much Edith could enjoy.

At a neighbor's suggestion Henry pulled back and waited for Libby to accept him. Little by little she came around, suborned

3

finally by a child's seat on the back of Henry's old Raleigh. They rode the bike up and down the ramps of a parking garage in Silver Spring with Libby barking to hear the echo. She loved having Henry hitch her on his hip with a big arm around her middle.

It was Henry who heard her cry, who picked her up when she fell out of the twin bed they'd given her. He would prop chairs and pillows between her and the dark chasm of the night. He was so sensitive to her movements in her sleep that he could tell two rooms away when she was sliding off. Once he caught her in mid-fall.

But she couldn't get into bed with him and Edith because Edith wouldn't allow it. Libby retaliated by refusing her own bed. It was the first real confrontation, passing through stages of increasingly sharp commands from Henry and some major-league screaming from Libby until finally he felt obliged to spank her bottom with his bare hand as his parents had done to him. Then she stayed in bed and, after some ritual yelling, fell asleep.

To defeat Edith became her prime objective. Perhaps its attainment was less enjoyable because it was so easy.

"Eat the peas," said Edith.

"No," said Libby. She had come equipped with this word.

"Eat your peas."

Libby dumped them on the floor. They damn well weren't *her* peas.

Edith scooped them back into the dish, set the dish just out of Libby's reach and told her she could leave the table when she consented to eat *her* peas.

Libby won that one at 11:15 p.m. Henry came home to find Edith asleep with her head on her arms and Libby wide awake in her booster chair with brimstone in her eye.

That a child two years old should have such power was more than Edith could bear. She had hoped that somehow the darling baby in the welfare department's photo would win her heart and help her overcome her antipathy to children. For a while she tried pretending Libby was a cat, and that helped somewhat, she told Henry. But in the end there would be peas and defeat again. Edith's ultimate response was to ignore Libby—stick her in her playpen or her room or the backyard and leave her to Providence and Henry.

Libby's siege weapon was the conventional tantrum— screaming, kicking, throwing what came to hand—but her attack weapon was what one startled guest called her black look, a glare of such intense hatred that the person besieged had to either assault her frontally or retreat. Henry was familiar enough with the tantrums but knew the black look only by hearsay. He dealt with the tantrums by battening the hatches to her room until the storm blew itself out. Spanking was reserved for felonious assault or sedition and was seldom necessary. Perhaps once in two months Libby seemed determined to escalate her tyranny until she got her bottom warmed. After it was over there would follow a period of sweet serenity. It was hard to believe her rage had been more than a bad dream.

Henry found corporal punishment such an effective backup weapon that he recommended it to Edith. "If she knows you'll spank her you almost never need to. You don't even have to threaten," he told her.

"You can do it because you love her," she said uncomfortably. He chose to ignore the implication.

It was preposterous to think Edith couldn't love Libby. It was almost a matter of definition. She was painfully conscientious about feeding the child, dressing her well, seeing that she was clean and healthy. Yet it was Henry who put her to bed, got her up, read to her, played with her, hugged her—and punished her when she forced him to it.

"She's not your child, she's your plaything," Edith told him after he'd carried her around to knock on doors at Halloween. He pointed out that it was Edith who'd gone to all the trouble to create the little witch's costume, exquisite in its detail beyond a child's needs. Edith was wonderful with a sewing machine. Henry found it encouraging.

"You should have been the one to go with her," he said. "You did all the work."

Edith said she never knew what Libby was going to pull.

"I've told you—all you need to do is spank her just once."

"I can't."

"Why not?"

"I'm afraid I'll kill her."

When Edith said such things Henry couldn't make himself believe it. He discounted them by ignoring them.

Then one day Edith left. She walked out on both of them. So Libby had lost her mother by winning her war. She developed asthma and a racking cough that kept her and Henry awake and irritable at night. It had never occurred to her that Edith could just give up and walk away.

Henry blamed it on the moving, that the house sale came through just at the wrong time so they'd had to bunk in with friends for an interminable month before their new house was available. He assumed that Libby was devastated and so became devastated on her behalf.

With Edith gone Libby clung to Henry all the more. For the first time since she'd started school that fall, she began to cry mornings when it came time to leave. Henry tried giving her a nickel a day to stop the tears and it seemed to work. How easy to bribe her—money for comfort at age six. But it bothered him, paying a child to swallow her tears, whatever the behavior modification theorists said.

At this time an almost pernicious flood of stuffed animals began. They were bought by Henry when he was obliged to make out-of-town trips. He started with bears of several sizes and hues—and sexes it appeared, judging by their raiments. Then came a serpent with green eyes and a blue mouth, a raccoon, a fox, a variety of limp dogs, an enormous turquoise walrus that Libby named Popsicle, and a monkey so real that Henry received strange looks when he carried it on the plane. Ostensibly these creatures were brought in return for a guarantee of good (or less than egregious) behavior while he was gone.

Mostly behavior wasn't a problem. If she didn't want peas Henry gave her peaches. He consulted her as he shopped and cooked. He permitted TV until nine. Sorting and filing clothes and toys was a joint venture. Given the choice of dusting or vacuuming she took the Electrolux because she liked the noise it made. She didn't get the rugs very clean, but she was playing a responsible role, Henry told her. He thanked a God whose existence he questioned that she was old enough to go to ladies' rooms alone.

When he was home, each of them was the other's prime companion for as many hours as she needed. Then she'd watch TV or play alone while he did desk work or read. When they took trips together her place was beside him, close as a girlfriend. Sometimes he felt like a marsupial. Dating was difficult. Women friends who met Libby were likely either to patronize her or to ignore her. Either way she would withdraw and smolder.

When her periods of outrageous behavior occurred, Henry tried to correlate them with his dating, but there seemed to be no pattern. It simply happened every two or three weeks. Libby would hurl herself against the walls of the establishment, violating treaties, smashing laws, defying all authority, reason, conciliation.

"It's time to go home, kiddo." After two hours at Candy Cane City, a recreation area in Rock Creek Park.

"No!" (Not "just a minute more." Not "oh, please.")

"Yes, sweetheart."

"No!" She climbed to the top of a slide in Olympian defiance.

*"Now,* Libby."

"No!" More shrill than the previous two. By this time everyone within fifty feet was aware of the drama, watching covertly. Henry bounded up the ladder in three steps, grabbed Libby more or less by the waist, tucked her under his arm, climbed carefully back to earth—no mean feat with a healthy first-grader. If there was no applause from the scattered audience, there was a certain transfixed admiration.

When she caught her breath Libby responded like a maiden mortified. She had a peculiar way of opening her jaws very wide, silently for a moment, then issuing screams of an intensity dangerous to adult ears.

Henry strode toward the parking area, doing his best to pretend his burden was a picnic basket. Libby kicked. She squirmed. She grabbed a section of Henry's belly and bit. By now everyone within five hundred yards was staring.

Henry stopped at a picnic bench, sat, upended Libby over his knee and swatted her well three times, stood her on her feet and marched her—weeping now, not screaming—to the car. As they drove away he saw out of the corner of his eye the shocked faces of three older ladies, and a man in faded fatigues with sergeant's stripes giving him the A-OK sign.

Two minutes later Libby was curled up against him with her head on his arm. Usually this transfiguration took an hour or more, but today's exorcism had been unusually vigorous.

Such events had happened rarely during Edith's reign. Now they were as predictable as the tides. Libby would start with a misdemeanor, then escalate steadily until Henry's mediative skills and patience dissolved. Often she picked a day when there was a great deal else to do and only the smallest time available for childish diversions.

"Come on, honey, finish your breakfast. We've got to go help the Millers load up the truck."

"Why are they moving?"

"I'm not sure. It doesn't matter. Hurry up, now." Henry was around the corner in the kitchen, absorbed in washing saucepans. Ten minutes later when he remembered to harass her, she hadn't moved. Her eggs were cold.

"Libby!"

Libby jumped.

"Do you want your breakfast or not!"

"Yes!"

"Then eat it!"

In another five minutes the eggs were in the garbage and Libby was ascending the stairs in a nasty frame of mind, under orders to dress, wash, and make her bed or be left behind alone. Henry, shaving in the bathroom downstairs, was uncomfortably aware of his tactical error. He couldn't leave her alone. Unthinkable. Perhaps she wouldn't notice.

Dream on, Henry. Your child has the greatest military mind since Patton.

Time marches. Ten minutes.

"Libby!"

No response. Henry knew better than to call a second time. He knew where she was and what she was doing. He stormed up the stairs. She was still in her pajamas, sitting on the edge of her bed staring out the window.

"Elizabeth Ann Calef!" (*Cannon to the left of us . . .*)

She shifted her gaze to the floor.

"Get your damn clothes on this minute!" (*Cannon to the right of us . . .*)

"I don't want to go." (*Into the jaws of death . . .*)

Henry pulled off her pajamas, yanked sweater and jeans onto her body, jammed her feet into sneakers. She stood upright, limp, a commandeered noodle.

"Go brush your teeth!"

She turned her head in the direction of the bathroom.

"Move!"

She took one step. She took another step. She took a third step.

Henry lifted her by the armpits, carried her to the sink. Squirted Gleem onto the brush. Placed the brush in her hand—then, in a brilliant tactical shift, kissed the back of her neck and went downstairs without another word.

Five minutes later there was no change in status. If the water had run, Henry hadn't heard it. He called her name cautiously up the stairwell, expecting no answer, receiving none.

With a deep sigh he slowly ascended, making plenty of noise about it. Libby was not in the bathroom but water *was* running, over the edge of the sink she had stoppered, onto the floor, perhaps enough already to stain the ceiling below. With a bellow he leaped to shut it off, then to Libby's room where she sat in the center of carefully orchestrated chaos. Sheets and blankets balled up in the corner. Drawers pulled from their sockets, contents strewn.

Breathing through his teeth, he tried to contain himself. They had been due at the Millers' twenty minutes ago.

"Okay," he said evenly. "I'm going downstairs to call Mr. Miller. I'm going to tell him why we're late—that we may not come at all, although I promised him and he's counting on me. Then I am going to bring the mop and you are going to clean up this entire mess, here and in the bathroom, if I have to stand over you all day and all night and all day tomorrow."

Feeling foolish and helpless he retreated down the stairs, called the Millers to say apologetically that he had a plumbing crisis, then reascended, mop in hand. Libby was sitting on her haunches in the middle of her minefield.

"Get up," said Henry.

She did not speak. She didn't have to. She gave him her black look, full voltage, obscene in its defiance, electrifying in its impact, adult, sexual, strident, insulting to the roots of Henry's heart.

Hardly aware of his own movements, he yanked her up, sat himself on her bed, turned her over his knee, pulled down her pants and spanked her until her sweet bottom was maraschino pink. He left her crying where she had dumped herself in a corner by the wall like the motherless child she was, and slunk down the stairs in defeat.

He sat at the dining room table over a bitter cup of guilt. Upstairs he could hear her struggling with the mop.

## 2. Henry and Margo

Henry could not embrace a woman without falling in love with her at least to a moderate degree. The syndrome seemed to originate not from his loins so much as in his hands. If he became intimate enough with her so as to trace her eyebrows gently with his fingers or to caress the skin of her temples he began to get indentured. It was as though there were an electrical circuit from the tips of his fingers to his heart. If the woman in question had long hair that might be fondled, it was perilous for Henry even to encounter her in a gas station.

Henry met Margo in Funkhouser's Garage in Midland, Virginia. She had long dark hair with copper highlights in the September sunlight, a long body, and a long neck. (Henry had never met a woman who did not think her neck was too long or too short.)

Margo was dressed in mud-stained jeans, a faded blue farm shirt, Red Wing high-top work boots. She looked at the world through the bright, deep eyes of a sprite. She was leaning on the garage doorway waiting for her Jeep wagon, holding a six-week-old German shepherd puppy in her arms.

When Henry looked at her she said hello. Her smile was friendly but not provocative. Without being aware of it Henry assumed she had money. (Later it turned out that she knew people with money. She was simply comfortable in herself, full of the power of a woman in her mid-thirties.)

Henry at this time was fifty years and six months old, in his second year as sole parent of Libby, now seven. After two failed marriages and a disastrous affair with a woman from Missouri, he had given up on love, except only for this adopted child whom he carried everywhere like a pearl in a saucer, aware as he did so that the two of them were appealing and perhaps overly cute, like a Shirley Temple movie or a Tatum and Ryan O'Neal movie or any story about an attractive man and a spunky little girl struggling with the taciturn galaxies. It all nauseated him a little, but he didn't see what he could do about it.

From his second marriage to Edith, Henry had salvaged a run-down farm near Sumerduck, Virginia, where he still took Libby on weekends to escape from Washington's unbreathable congestion. On the Saturday when he met Margo he had with him a second seven-year-old neighbor to keep Libby company. If the girls were unaffected by Margo's warmth, they were captivated by the puppy she held. Henry asked if they might pat it.

*Meet cute,* he thought, scowling to himself, but Margo was unaware of such niceties. She liked the little girls. She was glad to share her puppy. She was comfortable making small talk with Henry. Within the first five minutes he knew her husband had been killed in an air crash, that she lived near a village called Calverton with three children, that she rode to the hounds, that she had fallen from her horse into the swamp this morning and had never expected to meet somebody new looking like this.

Henry let it be known that he was neither obligated nor married, was father of one, not both, of the girls, and worked for the government.

Her Jeep was ready; his car would be tied up until mid-afternoon. She brought him and the girls home for lunch, talking the whole way with a strand of her hair caught in the rolled-up window. He was so disturbed by it that he had trouble hearing what she was saying. Finally, compulsively, he pointed it out.

"Oh, that," she said. "It keeps happening. I'm such a flake. I should have all this hair cut off."

"Oh, please don't," Henry heard himself saying, angry that he had made a personal remark so soon, but thinking then that she had made the overture, and wishing finally that he could have made his response sound more like a courtly sophisticate's and less like that of a hair fetishist in disarray. He even considered amending the remark in an effort to diminish it by expanding it when he realized that it was all long forgotten. Margo was talking to the little girls about ponies. Would they like to ride one?

Libby, who feared nothing physical, would love it. Amy, the visitor, was leery but fascinated.

Margo's house was full of air and light—an expanded A-frame with fourteen-foot ceilings and a wall of windows that looked out over a deck to a pasture with horses, then to sweeping fields of corn. In the distance a Conrail freight howled for a grade crossing.

Margo herself was full of air and light, trying to make lunch and talk, running out to the barn to get the pony, laughing at her own disorganization. What did Henry do for the government? she asked.

He thought through the chaos of his bureaucratic workdays. "Well, I guess you could say I'm a planner."

"A planner! Lord, I don't know what I'm going to do from one day to the next"—she broke off laughing—"from one minute to the next."

She handed him a hamburger, juicy, sweet as filet. She had a high, prominent bottom. Henry tried not to look except when her back was turned. She fed the little girls hot dogs, then took them out, sat them on the pony and led it around a fenced ring with cavalletti and several small hurdles in it.

"I teach riding to kids—some a lot younger than this," she called from the far side of the enclosure. She talked all the time, to Henry, to the girls, to herself.

"Where are your own kids?" Henry called.

"Church day camp. They should be along any time now."

The pony followed Margo around and around, oblivious to its giggling passengers. It reminded Henry of a railroad tank car— same color, same proportions.

Margo told him she also worked as a hostess at Airlie House, the convention and training center near Warrenton. An hour later she confessed to having stretched the truth. "I'm really just a bartender. Whatever will bring in money. I paint pictures of people's horses. I don't have any real skills except with horses. I was a sheltered wife. My neighbors had to come help me do my checkbook and collect my insurance and pay the bills. I had to sell Craig's Monte Carlo and his hunter, Brandy, to pay off the credit cards. You should have seen Brandy—" She stopped suddenly. Turned and went into the kitchen. "More coffee?" she called after a minute.

"Someday we'll get married," Henry said, and immediately wished the words back. The poor woman was still struggling with her loss, and here he was playing with her affections.

Margo laughed. "Wait till you meet my kids."

What Margo gave Henry was joy. At that age she knew what she was—a mother, a lover of nature and God's creatures (except the groundhogs that dug the holes that felled the horses that threw the riders), a lusty woman who loved getting up to greet the day because it smelled good and would be full of surprises, who loved going to bed at night because she loved sleeping and she loved loving. She told Henry her two favorite things were done in bed, then was horrified when he quoted her. "You make me sound lewd."

She bullied her children and smothered them with affection. Henry was startled to hear her threaten to break Thomas' arm, then demand a kiss before he went to bed. "I yell at my kids. I probably shouldn't. Probably everything I do for my kids is wrong, but they know I love 'em and that's what counts in the end."

Everybody was gladiatorial. Marty, the fifteen-year-old, was wiry, undersized, excessively courteous, remote. His aggressiveness came out on the tennis court when Henry tried to play with him and couldn't score a point in four games. Marty was ruthless, his serves only marginally less than lethal. "You're frighteningly good," Henry told him. It was the first time Marty smiled—but a secret smile, his head half-turned.

Thomas made everything a competition. "What's the best

car going?" he asked Henry when they met. "Mercedes?" "Wrong. Try again." "Jaguar?" "Wrong. Try again." "I give up." "Lamborghini." Thomas was nine. "What's so good about it?" Henry said. "Don't," said Margo, "unless you've got all week." "I'll give you a book," Thomas said.

"I'm going to play for the Cowboys," Thomas said.

"Not the Redskins?"

"The Redskins suck."

"Thomas!" said Margo.

"You wanna arm wrestle?" said Thomas.

Henry had not realized what a strange age thirteen is in girls until he spent an hour alone with Sandra. This was three weeks after he had met Margo, had taken her to the Kennedy Center, wangled one delicious night with her at his house in Washington and two uncomfortable nights alone on her couch in Calverton. Margo was terribly concerned about what the children would think, especially Sandra, so that when Sandra transparently manipulated time alone with him to shop for crabs he took her along with some interest. She was nothing if not direct. Two hundred yards down the road she said, "There are some things I felt I ought to warn you about before you marry into this family."

"Who said I was going to do that?"

"Well, aren't you?" she said with such outrage that he ran for cover.

"It's a possibility, but not soon."

"All right. So much for that. Here's what you should be aware of. First, my older brother is a bank robber, my mother is crazy, and Thomas waits a whole week to go to the bathroom, then plugs up the toilet."

16

She stopped speaking and stared at him, calculating the effect. Clearly a humorous response would be out of order. Henry concentrated on the road.

"Wow," he said.

"It's true. Every word of it."

"Can we take these things one at a time? What's this about Thomas?"

"Thomas tries to be the most disgusting person who ever lived. He eats mashed potatoes and gravy and then opens his mouth to make me sick."

"But about the going to the bathroom?"

"He actually waits up to a whole week. Deliberately. Then he does this huge *thing* in the toilet and leaves it for me. You can't even flush it down or the toilet will back up and spill all over the floor. I go crazy when it happens. Daddy used to make him clean it up because it happened every week, but Momma just shakes her head and takes care of it herself. Momma spoils both the boys and is very hard on me."

"And Marty robs banks?"

"It's true. Every word of it. He and Leslie Goldthwaite, the minister's son, held up the bank in Catlett and Marty got caught by the FBI before he could count the money. I can show you the newspapers."

"When was this?"

"Three years ago."

"He was twelve and he robbed a bank? How's he been doing since?"

Sandra searched Henry's face carefully. Finally when no trace of smile appeared she continued. "Ahh—he just goes off and plays tennis all the time and won't do a thing around the house. Momma lets him get away with it."

In hope of steering clear of Sandra's concept of Margo's

craziness, Henry diverted the conversation to Sandra herself. It proved to be an acceptable substitute. She said she was an abused child.

Henry considered this for a moment. If Thomas' bowel movements were an open topic—what the hell. "You mean sexually abused."

Sandra's eyes widened. "Oh, no!"

"Physically, then. You get beaten."

"You're ridiculing me! You're like all the rest of them."

"Not at all," he said straight-faced. "You said you're abused. I was seeking clarification."

"I'm emotionally deprived," she said staring out her window. "And I don't think I want to discuss it right now."

So they discussed Henry's bachelor fatherhood and his house in Washington and his old farm in Sumerduck. He tried unsuccessfully to explain what a bureaucrat does with his days.

"That's all right." Sandra patted his arm. "Some things are too subtle to put into words, aren't they."

# 2

---◆◆---

Henry and Margo had much to discuss in this April of their friendship, when mutual flattery falls as gently and frequently as spring showers. Henry loved the sound of her voice so much that he ran up a $100 phone bill calling her from Washington the first month he knew her. It didn't matter much what she said. The fact was that she laughed easily and talked easily so that Henry felt he was doing so, too, when in reality he was simply smiling and listening, vicariously riding her roller coaster.

She made him feel good about himself. When she told him he was attractive he was afraid to believe it but wisely didn't argue. When she told him he was kind he was able to accept it because he knew he tried to be kind. When she admired his driving he swelled up like a major because he knew it was true. With difficulty he limited his response to five minutes. When she said he was a wonderful lover he melted. "It's you," he said. "You excite me so much."

"You have wonderful hands," she said. "I look at them and think what they do to me and I feel sexy all over."

But loving continued to be constrained by the children. "They get upset if I'm not home by midnight."

"I can make love at seven," he told her.

Even this was difficult — getting time alone with three chaperons weighing Margo's excuses like cynical traffic cops.

"Anyhow, I don't love you just for your body," he said, which was true except that her bottom still drove him crazy.

She got him on a horse, crowed when he posted a few strides the first time out, led him through the woods at a heart-stopping clip. But her hair flew ahead of him in the twilight and he had no choice but to follow. After the first two falls it was less terrifying.

She caught him taking Rolaids. "I have a cure for that," she said looking smug.

"Oh? What?" He'd had a motherful of advice on this subject.

"Yelling."

"Yelling. Well . . ." They'd just finished a mellow dinner at a country inn and were driving by November moonlight to Henry's old farm to make love by the fireplace. "November is the Hunter's Moon," he said.

"You're changing the subject."

"Yelling drives me crazy."

"Because you hide from it. I've watched you with the kids. You're very patient, but you're storing it all away. Then you take Rolaids. Why don't you get it out?"

"Because I'll say something I'll regret. I'm getting irritated right now. Why do we have to do this?"

"I'm making you irritated. I'm digging at you. Say it. Whatever it is, say it."

"Okay. I think your theory is simplistic. I think you need more self-control with the kids. You yell at them and it doesn't mean a thing. Nobody pays any attention to you."

There was a long wounded silence. She had never hidden in silence before. It was their first serious argument in two months

together. Henry felt as though he'd clubbed her. He reached out a
tentative hand for her knee.

"They know I love them," she said finally. "That's what
counts."

"And they love you. I just hate to see them use you." Henry
couldn't surrender his point even in reconciliation.

She put her head on his shoulder. "I suppose I'm a terrible
mother."

"You're a wonderful mother. I'll try to yell more."

Margo giggled.

He told Margo that the only stable years Edith had were the ones
with him.

"And yet she left you," Margo said.

"She couldn't cope with motherhood."

"She couldn't cope with Libby. It's not the same thing. Libby
stole you from her. I'm not sure I can cope with Libby myself.
She's my chief rival, you know."

"She's got to get over hanging on me" was his response.

Loving by the fire at the old farm was wonderful but cold. The
fireplace had been designed to give cheer without warmth. It
sucked heat from the room. Margo and Henry were wrapped
tightly in his bedroll on the floor, drifting in and out of sleep.
The farm was isolated, a mile from the nearest dwelling. Moonlight poured in the windows, seemingly from all directions at
once, filling the room.

"Did you and Craig yell at each other?"

"It was how we communicated. It's very different with you. All kinds of stuff goes on under the surface."

She was silent then for another long period—not rigid but withdrawn, even in his arms.

"I've never told you about that night I got the phone call from the coroner. I kept asking him if he was sure until finally he had to tell me there'd been a fire. It was April 4 and blowing hard all night. Somehow the wind made it darker, as though the whole earth had turned barren. I kept turning lights on but the darkness wouldn't go away, so finally I turned them all off and let it be dark. I went out to the barn to check the horses, and suddenly I felt Craig's hand on my shoulder, as though he'd come home to help me be strong for the children. But I couldn't at first. I went up to bed and listened to that terrible wind, and I shook all over the rest of the night and the next day. Off and on for weeks the shaking would come back and I'd have to get drunk to make it go away."

He held her tightly as though his warmth could diminish the memory. Twice more in the next few weeks she repeated the story almost verbatim, unaware she had told him before.

When he mentioned it she was distressed. "You'll think I'm asking for sympathy." She distrusted pity—it placed the one pitied in a taking position, she said. "Strong love needs equal footing."

"You've had a lot of pain to deal with. You have to work it out."

"What I'm dreading is the holidays. I tell myself I've got things pretty well under control, but Thanksgiving is next week. His birthday is December 4. Then there's Christmas."

"Can't I help? It's not a question of feeling sorry for you. And I certainly don't want to push my way in where the kids are concerned. But mightn't a male presence at Thanksgiving be helpful? I do have a holiday problem with Libby, you know."

It was dusk on a winesap afternoon, brushed with the pumpkin colors of Indian summer, muted with a smoky haze over fields and clusters of trees that stood black against the sky. Henry and Margo were walking their horses home down a winding gravel road. The land smelled like a good saddle. It was the sort of afternoon that made Henry wonder if he was in love with Margo or Virginia.

"That would work, you know—about Thanksgiving. If we can be giving you and Libby something . . . That was the hardest thing when Craig died—having to take help when I was helpless and couldn't do anything in return."

So it was reciprocating that made the difference. Margo, who loved to cook and did it well, proved to be a planner when it came to feast time. Sandra took Libby in tow in a conspicuous display of generosity, giving her lessons on the pony, taking her trail riding. The night before Thanksgiving Libby reported they'd taken a shower together and drawn pictures in the soap on each other's backs. And Henry and Thomas inadvertently created a new derivative of baseball.

They were playing catch, up and down the length of the riding ring, a distance roughly comparable to that between the pitcher's mound and home plate. "Throw it harder," said Thomas.

Henry zipped one in and had the satisfaction of a healthy thwack in Thomas' glove.

"Harder," said Thomas, snapping it back. "Put some steam on it."

Henry threw it harder, but with restraint. This was, after all, a nine-year-old boy. Thomas handled the throw neatly, spun, rifled it back again.

"All you got," he said from a crouch. "Show me some stuff."

Henry wound up thoughtfully. This was to be a serious game. All games were serious with Thomas. This boy was so full of team spirit that he constituted a team all by himself—this boy, who had discreetly sent word through Libby that he didn't want to be called Tommy or any other diminutive, then or ever after.

"How do we know who wins?" he called.

Henry stopped the windup, conscious that Marty had come out onto the porch to watch at a distance. "First one who makes ten errors loses," he said. He wound up again and blasted the ball at Thomas with his arm, shoulder, rib cage, heart, and his whole mind.

Thomas caught it, bobbled it, hung on, his honor at stake. "Wow!" he said. And a minute later, "What did you say the name of this game was?"

"Ten Errors."

"Ken Evers?"

"No, dummy," said Marty from the porch. "He said Ten Errors."

But it was Ken Evers then and forever thereafter, named in memory of the fabulous mythical Red Sox slugger with the eighty-one-millimeter arm, who could throw a strike from far right field in Fenway Park to home plate.

The next day, after Thanksgiving dinner, Henry ran over the dog. Not the puppy, but Admiral, the revered, elderly poodle of great IQ, who was so old and deaf that he lay under Henry's Oldsmobile and let Henry back over him at one mile per hour.

"Oh God," said Henry, who was always careful with animals. "How is he?"

Margo crouched over Admiral. "We'd better get him to the vet," she said. "Bring the Jeep over here so we can lift him over the tailgate."

"Oh God, I'm so sorry. I've never hit a dog before."

"Just be quiet, will you, and bring the wagon."

Admiral did not cry out but lay dazed on the ground, a drop of red at the corner of his mouth, while Henry stared at him in horror. Only when Margo stood up in exasperation could he move to get the Jeep. Together they lifted the dog gently into the back where Margo rode with him while Henry followed her directions to the veterinarian's home office.

Several more times on the way he tried to express his dismay at what he had done, but Margo's response was perfunctory. Finally she almost snapped at him.

"Please stop that. I understand that you feel bad. I know you mean well. I don't blame you for what happened. But I don't have what it takes to deal with your emotions. I've got all I can handle of my own this year."

*I know you mean well*—the ultimate put-down, the E-for-Effort. Henry sat alone in the car, while in the office Margo and the vet (obviously an old friend) discussed Admiral's fate. Eventually she came out and sat in the passenger's seat. Henry, silently grateful she'd left him to drive, headed toward her home.

"The dog could be saved," she said after a minute or two, "but I told him not to try. It would just prolong what the kids have to deal with. That's why I got the puppy."

"I feel like an ogre."

Margo turned and looked at him thoughtfully. "You've got to stop that, you know," she said gently. "It only makes it worse. I'm sorry if I snapped at you back there, but you're playing the wrong role. You keep saying I ought to marry you and I've taken it as a form of flattery. But if I'm going to consider it seriously I have to know you're strong. I can't take on a new set of problems."

It took Henry several hours to digest this. Finally, late that evening they sat before the fire. The kids were all in their rooms. Margo put her head on his shoulder. "I do love you," she said. "You have a good heart. You do mean well."

"Don't say that."

"But you do. You try to be a good person."

"What you imply is that trying isn't enough."

"I'm sorry. I didn't mean it that way."

Henry put his arms around her. "I can't make guarantees," he said quietly. "I'm a used truck. I've been through a couple of bad wrecks. But I can still haul a lot of furniture, except maybe this metaphor, which is getting kind of heavy."

"You always have to do it, don't you?"

"Do what?"

"Put yourself down."

"Do I?"

"You're a wonderful, kind, generous, strong, and attractive man."

"You're not consistent."

"I'm not?"

"You were just complaining that I'm not strong enough."

"I was?"

Margo took the children to New Orleans for Christmas to be with her family. "It's going to be bad without Craig no matter what we do," she said to Henry's suggestion that they get through it together. "There's no sense in our spoiling it for you."

So they had a brief pre-Christmas dinner at which Henry

gave her children gifts just expensive enough to make them uncomfortable, he realized too late: a portable typewriter for Marty (never used), a six-foot styrofoam glider for Thomas (crashed that day), and a sequined sweater that Sandra dutifully wore when he came—so consistently that Henry was sure it was never otherwise used. But everyone was politely grateful, coming, seriously, to hug him—startling to Henry whose Yankee customs didn't include being hugged at all, much less by boys. That and being called "sir." It felt almost hostile to him at first, the way you had to address an officer in the Army.

Late that night (it was the 20th) Henry and Margo exchanged a silver bracelet for a pair of riding boots (another surprise) and sat more tranquilly before the fire than either of them would have thought possible.

"I actually feel peaceful," she said.

"So do I."

"I'm almost sorry we're leaving."

"You could change your mind."

"Not really." She struggled up from the depths of the couch to add a log to the fire and fuss with it—successfully, Henry noticed.

"That's a good blaze," he said.

"It's not that I don't love you. You do understand that."

"Yes."

"I think it would be a good thing to marry you. I know it would." She glanced at him over her shoulder. "I want it to be more than a good thing. I want it to be wonderful. I want to be sure."

"It's never sure."

"I want to see how much I miss you when we're apart. I mean . . . I know I'll miss you, but I want to see if it's unbearable. Do you understand?"

"Like finding the perfect fur in the first store but being compelled to check all the others?"

There was a silence. She was beside him again, his arm around her shoulder, but she was holding herself in. "That was nasty."

"It was not. How? What was nasty about it?"

"I do not"—she struggled forward on the couch—"perceive you as something on a rack. A pelt. You will find no furs in my closet, incidentally. I don't wear dead animals."

"I was just being funny."

"It wasn't funny if it made me feel bad. I'm just trying to make the most important decision of my life."

"More than marrying Craig?"

"When you're that age you don't make decisions. You think you do, but you don't. Maybe your body makes decisions: eat, make love, choose a mate, have babies. So now I want it to be me."

"That's not quite what you were saying five minutes ago."

"I'm not responsible for five minutes ago. I'm responsible for now. Here's what I'm going to do. I'm going to ask you not to call me when we're in New Orleans. I want to test myself to see if I can stand it without you. When I can't stand it I'll call you."

"This is a test of the intellect?"

"Who said anything about the intellect?"

"What was all that business about making decisions? Using your mind instead of your heart."

"You weren't hearing me. What I said was, I want to listen to my heart instead of my body."

To Henry's male and Yankee mind such stuff was a distinction without a difference, but finally now that he was fifty he was wise enough to accept it as her logic if not his own. He saw them off at Dulles International and drove back to Washington feeling empty, the more so for Libby's presence.

Next morning Margo called. "This is not a call," she said. "This is just letting you know we arrived safely."

"I'm glad you cleared that up for me."

"Don't be such a Yankee."

"I'm not. I'm smiling because your voice makes my ear happy."

"When I come home I'll make you happy all over."

"Does that mean you think we should get married?"

"I probably won't decide until the minister asks me. You know how I am."

"I'm beginning to."

# 3

———— ·•· ————

This was their betrothal. They spent the next few months getting to know family and friends.

Courting the whole family, Henry did his best to get through Marty's reserve, but the response was never more than polite. He looked Henry directly in the eye, answered when spoken to, called him "sir" on every possible occasion. All of these things Henry took to be signs of veiled hostility, notwithstanding Margo's insistence that it was because her children had been brought up to respect their elders.

Certainly compared to Libby, who was going through a particularly exasperating phase of sullenness that year, Marty had superb manners.

"But it still puts me off to be called 'sir' all the time as though I were a lieutenant colonel who'd been promoted because he knew somebody."

"You can't help yourself. You chilly Yankees were never brought up to be courtly."

It was said with a smile, but Henry was sour. "You always say that. Just because Libby and I don't run to kiss everyone who walks in the door."

Margo shrugged. "Which way is nicer?"

Nobody won these debates, of course, but it still irritated Henry to have Marty look at him hard and say "yes, sir," and then ignore what he was asked to do.

So he wasn't asked to do much. The fact that he had robbed a bank was so spectacular that anything approaching conventional behavior was accepted with a sigh of relief by his mother.

Tennis was Marty's obsession. It provided a legitimate way for him to try to kill people and stay legal. He won trophies for it.

His joy was in jousting. If there was a way he could accept comfort, he hid it well. Watching, Henry couldn't believe there wasn't a pain center buried deeply somewhere. But such a person wearies all who must live with him.

At the beginning, Henry had assumed that Marty was remote because he saw himself as man of the family in his father's place and thus could be expected to have no use for a prospective stepfather.

"Might it provide a light touch," he suggested to Margo, "if I went to Marty and asked him for your hand?"

Margo thought it would be sweet, but she was wrong. It was awful. Whether he thought Henry was laughing at him or because he cared too deeply to handle it with a light touch, Marty was knocked over by the question.

Henry had sought him out in his private lair off the cluttered basement rec room with its Ping-Pong table buried in part of a wash, horse blankets, barbells, and other stuff the kids had dumped on their way upstairs. The contrast as Henry entered Marty's room was remarkable. He had made a cell for himself. The walls were purple. On the window panes he had painted a representation of steel bars. There was a cot, a bookcase, a dresser, and a fifty-gallon fish tank that provided the room's only illumination at the moment. An invisible radio was playing Led

Zeppelin. Crosswise on the bed lay Marty staring at his brilliant tropical fish adrift in their own prison. Even in repose he looked tense. He reminded Henry of the elastic windings inside a golf ball.

Marty glanced up, moved just enough to make room for Henry on the edge of the bed. Together they stared at the fish.

"Salt or fresh?" Henry asked after a while.

"Salt."

"Tricky," said Henry.

"Not if you know what you're doing."

Another silence. The fish performed selections from *Giselle*. Henry went over his mental notes a last time.

"Addictive," Marty said.

"Mm?"

"The fish. They're like a habit, you know? I lie here and stare at them and pretty soon I'm in there with them." Hardly the opening for a formal proposal.

Henry made himself as comfortable as he could on his small corner of the bed, taking care that no part of their bodies should touch.

"Marty, I need to speak to you of earthly things for a moment."

Marty stayed lost in the tank.

"Okay?" said Henry.

"Okay."

"You may have noticed that I'm uncommon fond of your mother, and I'm sensitive to the fact that this household is your turf. You've been the man around here for more than a year now. I don't want to do anything to muscle in on you, but I would awfully like to marry her. So I'm making a point of coming to you to ask your permission. At the wedding I'd like you to be the one to give her away." He paused. "I promise to do my best to maintain her in the life-style to which she has become accustomed, sir."

During this speech Marty stared into the fish tank. When it was over he buried his face in his arms.

"Marty?"

No response. He wasn't crying. He was trying to de-exist himself.

"Marty?"

Marty took a deep breath, faced Henry. He tried to lock eyes with him but couldn't. He sat up on the corner of the bed away from Henry and stared down at his hands.

"You shouldn't ask me," he said. "She's a grown person. She can do what she wants." He clearly wished Henry would get out and leave him alone.

Henry stood. "I'm sorry if I upset you," he said softly. "I just wanted to include you in."

"I know."

Henry moved to the door. "I hope you'll be willing to give her away. She'd want that."

Marty lay flat on his belly again. Re-entered the fish tank.

———— ◆ ————

When his father crashed into a North Carolina mountain it was nothing like Marty's daydream, which was just a picture with the sound shut off. But the sound of a dead man's home was women weeping, heavy footsteps, doors banging—sounds that made Marty's stomach crumple.

Caught in the midst of it, Marty couldn't feel how he felt. It was as though God were watching him from the balcony over the kitchen, waiting to see if he would give away his complicity in his father's death. It was as though he himself were up on the balcony, watching himself down on the floor, until gradually his watched self disappeared and the watching self was all that was left, and nothing was left but the shell of Marty with nothing inside, sticking close to his mother, trying to do what she needed without getting in the way—through the surreal day after the midnight phone call, on the flight to Atlanta to his grand-mother's house for the funeral, being placed in charge of Sandra and Thomas who were behaving like wimps every step of the way.

Finally there was the going to the funeral home with his mother and his grandmother, who moaned to herself in the back seat, and when they met the funeral director she loudly de-manded an open casket for the wake until the man had to say what never should have been uttered, that there had been a fire, that the body had been delivered in a leather pouch, so that all through the wake Marty had to see the charred body inside the closed casket, and once he had to go find the bathroom to flush away the terror he felt, seeing himself as his father about to be smashed and broiled on the head of a cliff.

They'd put him to bed in what had been the maid's room in the basement of his grandmother's house. When he woke there was sunlight pouring in through the windows above his head. He climbed on a chair to see outside.

His eyes were at ground level. He was seeing the world from a grasshopper's-eye perspective. Even though the lawn had been new cut, it looked like a jungle from down here.

A bright spark of blue caught the corner of his eye, then faded when he looked directly at it. He moved his head slightly. The jewel disappeared but another sprang out to its right, a blazing sapphire, a point of light smaller than an ant's eye. Marty moved his head one millimeter. The sapphire turned jade, then ruby, then vermilion shading to orange. Then a second appeared, deep ultramarine, then another vermilion—fires in the jungle.

He hunched himself upward an inch and there were twenty new jewels beaming at him from what seemed to be all directions at once but really was a patch of sunlight no more than two feet across where a spike of light shot through the trees above. Marty realized the grass was turning hot, so hot that it was actually smoking up into the ray of sunlight. In a minute or two it would all be gone. He thought about calling Sandra to come see it but changed his mind. This was his.

From above came his mother's voice. Was he dressed yet? She couldn't hear him or wouldn't believe him so that he was obliged to climb down from the chair and go to the foot of the stairs where she could see him.

When she was finally satisfied, he'd hurried back to his window, but the sun that had created the magic had burned it up. Even the steam was gone.

Henry and Margo took a trip to New England in April to meet Henry's mother and brother. Margo was excited because she'd never been so far north before, but Henry was full of foreboding. The idea that a man might marry a third time was so outrageous that it could not even be discussed. The command visit to Newton was less a welcome to the prodigal son, Henry knew, than it was a firsthand opportunity for his mother to meet the occupants of a flying saucer. Yet the trip was truly a pilgrimage of penance for this fifty-year-old son—and perhaps an effort to show that this third marriage would not be to some southern floozy but to a lovely widow, mother of three. He had gone through a mental exercise of warning Margo not to tell Mother she worked as a bartender, then had given it up, preferring offense to his mother over offense to Margo, if there had to be a choice. Perhaps it wouldn't come up.

If nothing else, Henry's years of tortured communication with his mother had the effect of fine-tuning a sense of ironies so subtle that no one with a conventional tolerance for pain could even understand them, much less feel them.

When he was in his thirties Henry submitted to a personality inventory in an effort to delineate his unfocused anger. One item asked that he complete the sentence "The greatest influence in my life was ———." He had written "my father," hardly aware that it was a lie.

Fifteen years later when, after his affair with the woman from Missouri, he had encountered the same test with the same question, he'd said again that it was his father, but that time he knew it wasn't true. The answer should have been his mother.

Henry knew his mother was exultant each time one of his marriages broke up, though of course she professed nothing but concern and sympathy for both him and the wife in question and would have tearfully denied anything like the *Schadenfreude* she felt. But she did enjoy the dissolution of these marriages that had been consummated without her blessing. Henry knew it was true. She knew Henry knew it was true. Even more subtle was the question of the withheld blessing: she always anointed his marriages in word and gift while withholding her heart. Again, Henry knew and she knew he knew. When in time the brides came to know, the realization brought bitterness much deeper than Henry's because, although he suffered from it more than they, he had lived with it all his life and accommodated to it the way kangaroo rats adapt to the climate of the desert.

As they headed north from the Connecticut Turnpike to follow the river valley toward Hartford, masses of rocky promontories loomed above them like clenched fists, far different from the womanly roundness of Virginia. Henry felt a thrill of recognition in his spine, like Odysseus broken free from Calypso's island to deal with the harshness of the hostile world. This was how the earth should look, rock-strewn and craggy, a land that creates men and women who clench their fists in return to say, *We will supersede even the damned rocks, we will endure, we will clench our emotions to our bellies, endure one another, but endure, endure,* and Henry knew again what was the glue that bound him and his mother together—and his brother, Joey, and all the other flinty Yankees who never knew they had anything in common until they came out of the cold. He was coming home again.

Three hours later they parked before the massive stucco house where he had endured and survived his own adolescence. If it no longer looked massive to him, it was still a decent-sized house, even by Newton's standards—three stories tall with its first and second level porches to the west and the pergola and its wisteria vine at the east. Henry noticed that the wooden storm windows were still up, the awning fixtures still in place, that the paint on the sills and lintels and the framings was still white and fresh. Somewhere his mother had found a handyman.

Inside the vestibule the key was still behind the pillar where it had been hidden since 1938, but before Henry could use it the door was pulled open and there stood his formidable mother, less formidable now, round as a tea cozy, wrinkled, in a new gray wig, still wearing her pince-nez.

A shred of smoke slipped out the door over her head. "What's burning?" Henry said.

But she had to hug them, first Henry, then Margo, then Henry again, crooning into his ear in her happiness. Henry felt clamped.

"Something's burning!" he said. "Can't you smell it? Look—you can see the smoke. Good Lord—" He strode through the dining room, through the butler's pantry, into the kitchen, opened the oven, closed it again quickly to stop the cloud, turned off the burner. Margo looked around, grabbed two dish towels, dived for the oven, hauled out a blackened object about the size of a teddy bear in an aluminum pan. A roast. Formerly a roast. Henry remembered that his mother liked beef well done.

"Oh dear," she said peering at it. "Do you think we can save it?" Henry was striding about opening windows and doors. "You'll freeze us," she protested. "Do you know how much oil costs now?"

"Mother, the house is full of smoke. First we breathe, then we seek warmth. Couldn't you smell it?"

She sniffed cautiously. "I can now a little."

There followed a brief debate. Henry would take them out to dinner. Mother would save the beef. No resolution in sight. No matter. She had other things in mind. She took Margo by the arm and led her back across the hallway to the living room, where she had assembled her portraits. There were twelve paintings in all, on the couch, in each of the chairs, on the mantel, against the piano, one each leaning on the pilasters at the double doorway—mother's portraits from old photos—of her mother, her bearded father, her husband, her sons, her granddaughter Naomi, even one of Libby from a Christmas card.

As Margo moved about examining them, exclaiming in delight, Henry remembered he'd written to say she did some painting, too. There would be no need to evade the fact of her tending bar for her daily bread.

When Mother left them to reexamine the roast, Margo whispered, "She's good, Henry. This stuff is full of life."

"I know."

"Don't be so grudging. You bully her."

"I have to beat her to the punch," he said gloomily.

"How can you say that? She's a sweet little old lady!"

"You see? She's doing it to you."

Margo shook her head in mock disbelief. Henry was, she said, the kindest man she'd ever known, but he had no charity for his own mother.

Mother came back to say the roast was partly ruined but that she might be able to salvage half of it.

"Why don't we go out to celebrate?" said Henry in great and false cheer. "When's Joey coming?"

"Joey?"

"You said he'd meet us here."

"No, you're mistaken, darling. I distinctly told you we would drive up to see them."

"To New Hampshire?"

"Well, yes. That's where they live. They're very anxious to see you."

Henry was incredulous. "Mother, you never said anything of the kind. I've only got two days here. We don't want to spend it all on the road."

"Oh dear. I thought you had a week."

There followed a spirited debate about dinner. Only with great reluctance would Henry's mother abandon the roast. ("It was smoking, Mother—practically on fire.") She would not consider going out ("after you've driven all that way"). Henry must go out to Buxbaum's for sliced meats.

"Mother—Buxbaum's has been gone for ten years."

"Nonsense, I shop there every week."

This eventually was modified to "I send Tim with a list every week." Tim proved to be the faithful taxi driver who took her to church when she felt well enough, who horsed the storm windows up and down and replaced them with the awnings in summer, and who bought her groceries at the A & P when she sent him to Buxbaum's. As Henry left the house he noticed that Tim apparently clipped the hedge and mowed the lawn. Thank God for Tim when your mother is eighty. Henry also saw a new young elm tree growing from the stump of the old one, long lost to Dutch elm disease. *Endure,* he said to himself and went forth to buy a huge jar of Claussen's pickles at the grocery along with the meats and salads. Mother loved Claussen's. They'd be gone in two days.

When he arrived home again Mother and Margo were at the dining-room table digging through piles of old photographs—pictures of her own childhood, aunts, uncles, parents, the favorite dog Watch, pictures of Henry's own father and brother, and Mother in her forties looking like a dreadnought in her armor of embonpoint and her pince-nez, and Henry at three with his mass of curls.

"They were just the color of copper wire in the sun," Mother said. She reached for a last small packet, folded into a grimy copy of *Stars and Stripes*.

"You left these when you went off to college. I've been saving them all these years."

And there they were again, frozen for the camera with their silly grins—Laszlo, Captain Unruh, Lieutenant Epstein, Blanchard, Henry at twenty, Brioni, Samuelson, Sergeant Marsteller, Singwald, Hardesty, posed with the jeep and the .30-caliber water-cooled machine gun at the Marseilles railhead, faces half-lost in the sun's glare and the deep shadows of their helmets— their names listed on the back as though they would not sing in Henry's head forever, dated November 1944. Dead, all of them except Henry and Brioni and eyeless Laszlo after three hours of savage shelling in a hillside cabbage patch so sodden with November rain that digging in was hopeless and to rise and run only death. Oh, Mother, your timing is flawless. . . .

And Inara's letter, dated December 12, 1945:

My Dearest Henry,

I'm sleeping now, it is only 10:50 o'clock, but I can't fall asleep. I must think still long about you and about this night in the club.

To-day I was feeling very good, because I have hoped to meet you into the club. At the door from the club I was waiting for my girl-friend Vilna, and in this moment I met one soldier, with whom I have danced sometime in this club. He has said to me, that we must not stand outside and we went in and I was merry, that I can see you earlier. My Dearest, I'm sorry, I wanted to say this all self to you, but when you were dancing with on another girl, I couldn't do it, it was to late. And in this moment when I was with him in the club, I couldn't leave him in the first moment, because, he has taken me into. I could do it past 10 minutes, I know it wasn't good from me, but I can't do nothing more, I'm so anhappy, please, be not angry with me. I'm alone home, I could cry about all my life, I hope you will be good again, you will not leave me, but when yes, I can't think more.

Please say me the answer, can I see you again, or is it all by? Give me a short note with my girl-friend. I'm so waiting for you.

your Inara

In pencil, folded eight ways, some words almost lost along the creases. With a tiny snapshot of her seated on unknown steps, with a white flower in her hair (or perhaps a flaw in the print).

His first real love. She'd been Latvian, displaced, hustled from camp to camp. Home was a pallet in the corner of a room with seven other occupants.

Henry could remember no club, no dance, only his incredulous joy that a girl could love anyone so shy and lanky as he, the joy of making love in his sleeping bag, by day, by night, finally in a little room he'd rented by the Bahnhof for two packs of Camels a week. Because they made love in the room to the glow of an electric heater Henry had always loved electric heaters. In Latvian she'd taught him to count to ten and *es mīlu tevi.* Their language of love was made up of fragments of German, French, and English, laughing, playing with the words.

Then the unhappy ending: Henry called up out of turn with eight hours' notice to ship home, going at midnight to find Inara in the DP camp, taking her to a deserted square while she wept by a silent fountain in the December fog and the dark, saying goodbye forever, kissing her eyebrows, her eyes, her hair.

And coming home at last to a triumphant mother who had engineered his early departure with a sob story to the Red Cross.

> *mother, make my bed soon,*
> *For I'm sick at the heart, and I fain wald lie down.*

Henry and Margo were billeted not only in separate rooms but on separate floors, he in his old third-story bedroom, she in Joey's room next to Mother's.

But he went down anyhow, mindful of remembered treads that creaked, found her still awake under the blankets.

"Cold," she said. "If this is April, how do you stand the winter?"

He warmed her with his own body, wanting no more words, no more of the past, nor rage nor pain, wanting only now.

# 4

——◆——

They were married amid peonies in June, two months later. At the joint insistence of the family Marty soberly escorted his mother down the aisle of the little country chapel and donated her to Henry in the name of his brother and sister. There were many who wept at the sight.

If Marty wasn't among the weepers that day, he was at least back on his best behavior, shaking hands firmly, meeting eyes, mouthing the phrases of politesse.

A month or so before the wedding Henry had bumped into an old friend at a Washington party — a psychologist and mother of three. When he announced the glad tidings about finding Margo and her children, the friend was appalled. "Do you have any idea what you're getting into?"

"I already have one kid. What's a few more?"

"Henry, you have one sweet little girl. You're talking about taking on three roaring adolescents."

"I don't think Margo's children roar."

"All adolescents roar."

At the time Henry discounted the thought, but in the end it became a central element in his existence. He formulated a theory that he called the Adolescent Sleep/Stimulation Hypothesis, which said teenagers' circadian cycle demands sleep from 3:00 a.m. to 1:00 p.m. and intense stimulation for the rest of the day. If no external stimuli were present, the adolescents created their own by fighting. Males quarreled with females. The young warred with their elders. Brother fought with brother and sister with sister. In Henry's case there were the ready-made differences between the Bishops and the Calefs with Margo Bishop Calef caught in the cross fire.

Of all the words in the language there were none Margo the mother had come to dread more than *oops,* harbinger of disasters from smashed dishes to broken bones, followed by therapeutic yelling. Until Henry came.

From then on half of Margo's job consisted of shielding Henry from monsters. The other half was trying to help the children to love this kindly, remote Yankee she'd taken as her consecrated lover and their surrogate father. Henry could never have survived the way of life as it had been for Margo and the kids before, with aerial bombardment and heat-seeking missiles for breakfast.

It was not that the children disliked him. They just couldn't imagine that a man in his fifties might need love and acceptance from them. So she bought gifts and cards for everyone to give Henry on his birthday, Valentine's Day, Christmas, Easter, or whatever other occasion could be fabricated for warmth. On their first married Father's Day, all four of the kids and Margo woke him for breakfast in bed with coffee and a Ramos gin fizz and new sneakers and a red zippered sweat suit that cost four times what he would have spent. This last, she realized too late, made him uncomfortable. In fact the very celebration made him uncomfortable. As much as he secretly craved affection, he shrank before a scene, even a loving one.

These were family honeymoon days. When anyone had a nice word to say about anyone else, Margo made sure the message was carried. If there was a complaint she did her best to deal with it herself. The whole process amounted to her passing out a lot of love and absorbing a lot of anger.

Soon after Henry and Margo were married, Libby came down with shingles, easily diagnosed as transitional trauma. Margo was gradually weaning Libby from stuffed animals and onto real ones. Cats, dogs, a goat. A pony. Ultimately the shingles went away, and Libby disappeared into the pack of siblings and neighborhood kids. Henry hoped her need for restorative punishment would be absorbed in normal childhood rivalries.

He was aware of a lot of fights with Thomas that were more than half Libby's fault. Thomas was two years older, twice as big, but a terrible tactician. A Spanish bull of a tactician. Henry was grateful to him.

The Battle of Wounded Knee took place in the autumn after the wedding.

Henry had instituted a family system of allowances, labeled as wages for services required, but proportioned by need. As the youngest, Libby got a dime a week. The family was beginning to jell.

The knee wounded belonged to Thomas. A window had been broken in the basement. The combatants were so variegated that Henry, called in as arbitrator, despaired of sorting out roles. He kicked out all the other neighborhood kids and lined up his own four. He pointed out that he had repeatedly asked them not to roughhouse indoors. Told them he was severely disappointed. Swore a judicious amount. Said he was assessing no punishments since he was unable to assess culpability. Told them to watch the damn Redskins or whatever.

There was a silence.

"It was me," said Libby suddenly.

"What was?" said Henry.

"I broke the window. I threw the rock."

"Shut up, Libby," said Thomas.

"Shut up, Thomas," said Marty and Sandra.

"Be still, all of you!" shouted Henry. "It was everybody's fault. Now go outside! Go somewhere! Just behave yourselves."

When the others scattered, Libby stood alone crying uncontrollably.

"What, honey?"

"It was my fault."

"It's all right, honey."

"No!" She rushed down the stairs to her room, then up again, tripping over her feet. She ran to where Henry stood and slammed her fifty-seven-cent life's savings into his hand so violently that the coins scattered across the floor.


Libby always overestimated her own abilities. With blockheaded courage she bumped her way through childhood, charging into contests she had no way to win and getting dumped on her head. In her genes there seemed to be equal elements of perversity and indomitability. But these same traits helped to lock her into the family. When Sandra and Thomas gave her a crash course in cantering the pony she fell off five times in the first half hour, and climbed grimly back on five times—until Marty took pity on her and carried her into the house. She loved him instantly.

Loving Marty was easy for her because he was eight years older. The two-year interval that separated her from Thomas was altogether different. There was no way they could both be youngest child.

When Libby had said green was blue, Henry had always smiled indulgently and let it pass. But when she informed Thomas that green was blue he bellowed that it was a stupid thing to say and she was stupid for saying it. Blue was, by damn, blue, and she'd better get it straight. And then, of course, Libby had to say brown was blue, and Thomas would go through the roof.

"The word is not Jagwire, you idiot. . . ."

"You didn't jump four yards, you dummy. It was four feet. I can jump eleven feet. . . ."

"Mom, would you please make Libby wear a shirt."

"Why does *she* have to come, too?"

Libby was a hypodermic needle jabbing directly into Thomas' core, while he could hardly penetrate her hide. He could make her spit and scream, he could hurt her physically. But he couldn't wound her heart. She had it shielded, wrapped in lead.

At the beginning she wouldn't accept Margo's open invitation to be loved. She'd eaten her peas, helped with dishes, fed the ponies. But she wouldn't meet Margo's eye. More important, she wouldn't speak to her by name. She'd walk across the pasture rather than call to her. It went on for months.

Margo waited. "It's not that she's unresponsive," she told Henry. "And she's fitting in with the other kids—"

"Like four pairs of sneakers in the dryer?"

"—Okay, so they all thump around a bit. She may be the least trouble of the lot. But it bothers me that she won't give me a name."

"I'll talk to her about it."

"You stay out of it. This is between her and me. I want to pick a time when I can put some solid ground under her. This is a child who's learned not to trust women. She's been deserted by three—"

"Three?"

"The natural mother. Your Edith. The foster mother you snatched her from—"

"Snatched?"

"Well, whatever. You yourself told me how disoriented she was when you got her. And when she wanted to come to bed with you for comfort—as somebody had obviously encouraged her to do—your Edith banished her to a cold room."

"And I enforced it."

"Well, you were a shit, too," she said with a smile.

Margo gave Libby until Christmas to come around, then took her shopping to be alone with her. "The time has come," she said, "for me to have a name. I don't care what it is. It can be Margo. It can be Mom. It can be Auntie Booby—"

Libby giggled.

"—but it's got to be something. I've accepted you. Now you've got to accept me. Did it ever occur to you that it might hurt my feelings to be a no-name?"

It hadn't. Libby looked across the seat at her with enormous eyes.

"So what'll it be?"

Libby pursed her lips.

"Out with it."

Libby opened her mouth, then closed it.

Margo stopped the car in the middle of Route 28 and waited. A woman in the car behind them pulled around, glaring at them.

"Now," Margo said.

"I can't make it come out."

"You can."

"Mmph." A minimal sound.

"What?"

"Mom." Very softly.

"Louder."

"I can't."

"Pretend I'm Thomas. I just came into your room and borrowed your pillow without asking."

Libby giggled.

"I'm waiting."

Libby looked out the back window. It was a two-lane road. There were three cars waiting to get by. A truck was coming. A dump truck.

"We can't just sit here," Libby said.

The truck blew its horn a great redneck blat.

"Come on—" Libby said.

Margo reached for the key. Killed the engine.

"Mom!" Total outrage.

Margo started the engine, drove to Shakey's, bought a large pizza. Which they ate.

---

As fast as she decently could, Margo moved them out of the house where Craig Bishop had been father and husband, to a new farm near Broad Run where the family could all pitch in to bale and store the hay, fell the dead trees, and cut their own firewood.

Henry hated discord so much that he persuaded himself a family farm would have a great unifying influence and unite them all in a commonweal of sweat and wholesome achievement of the sort one sees in beer commercials.

When they moved from Calverton to the new farm, Marty claimed a basement room for himself and recreated his prison cell exactly as before.

What Henry did not realize until some time had elapsed after the wedding was that Marty was a pariah among his peers, who had casually tortured him all his life because he was always a little person swaggering to be big.

With Thomas and Libby he was aloof. They were too young to matter. With Sandra he was close about one week out of three. The rest of the time they fought. He would poach on her friendships, crash her friends' parties, behave badly, retreat in smoldering isolation.

"What can I do?" she complained to Margo and Henry. "He just comes barging in and drives me crazy. Last week he picked Peggy up by the crotch and the back of the neck and flipped her onto the couch."

"And?"

"He said 'Hi, Peggy.'"

By now Sandra was a sophomore in high school and Marty, having lost a year as a result of the bank-robbing episode, was a junior. The Peggy in question was a former neighbor who had grown up with them and teased Marty and fought with him like a cousin.

"Why doesn't Marty have his own friends in for a party?" Henry said.

Sandra and Margo stared at him.

"Have I said something absurd?"

"In the first place," Sandra said, "he doesn't have any friends. In the second place, you wouldn't want to invite his friends to this house. Besides, you don't know anything about parties."

"I don't?"

"Did kids get drunk at parties and get into fights and break up the furniture and go out on Route 603 and kill themselves at ninety miles an hour?"

"Well . . . not at the parties I was allowed to go to. But those things have been happening since the Roman Empire, baby."

"I bet you didn't have rednecks who spend their weekends cruising around sniffing out parties to crash. I bet you didn't smoke dope or some of the other stuff that goes around this county. You know the kids in the parking lots that make you mad? The guys with the ponytails and the pickup trucks?"

"Surely there must be a way to keep the Mongols out. Armed guards at the doors, perhaps?"

"What if I made a nice punch instead of just having beer?" Margo said.

"I'm not sure we should allow any beer at all," Henry said.

"Maybe you could invite the minister," Margo said.

Sandra covered her ears. "Come on, you guys!"

The ground rules, as finally negotiated, were as follows:

1. The party would be given jointly by Sandra and Marty;
2. Beer would be permitted in moderation. Drunks would be put to bed or chauffeured home;
3. No drugs;
4. Maximum capacity—forty persons;
5. No sex (interpreted as no overt sex);
6. Gate-crashers would be excluded by Marty and Thomas and three other football players;
7. An adult would be permitted to pass among the young every forty minutes.

Items Henry and Margo forgot in the package were lumens and decibels.

One of Henry's significant contributions to the combined household had been a pair of Seeburg disco speakers, each about the size of a four-drawer filing cabinet. Their reproduction was so faithful that he could close his eyes and be in the Kennedy Center picking out each woodwind and bowed bass note. He had never needed to use more than 10 percent of their power.

Because they were so large, the only place for them in the Broad Run house was the basement rec room where they were an instant success. With the volume at three-quarters, a Rolling Stones record turned the floors, walls, the very joists and rafters into an enormous sounding board from which there was no escape. The kids loved it, and were promptly told they could play it only when the adults were out of the house.

At 6:30 on the evening of the party the speakers were given a trial run. Upstairs Henry tried the television. He couldn't hear a bit of it.

"I'm going to have to lip-read the news," he shouted to Margo. "How long did we say they could go?"

"Till one."

"Would you mind if I slept in the barn?"

"You'll stay right here with me and endure it. This party was your idea."

"I'm prepared to deny that."

"Have you seen the decorations?"

"What are they?"

"Two very small purple light bulbs."

"My God. They won't be able to find their way to the bathroom. Did you make them leave the regular bulbs in the overheads in case of fire or civil disorder?"

"No. You'd better check."

Henry checked. The bulbs had been removed. He put them back and told Sandra not to touch them on pain of death.

"Somebody will keep turning them on to bug people," she complained.

"Hide the switch. Put one of the speakers in front of it." Henry retreated up the stairs as Mick Jagger obliterated the sound of human voices.

By ten o'clock Henry was pacing the floor.

"Only three hours to go," Margo said sweetly.

"Why are they all screaming?"

"They're trying to communicate over the music. I think it's your turn to do patrol duty."

"What's the use? You can't see anything."

"They can see you. That's important."

Libby, who was still too young to participate, had been up and down on spy missions. "Somebody brought rum," she reported.

"Much of it?"

"Just one, I think."

"Does anybody seem to be drunk? Is anyone smoking pot?"

"I don't think so. Not yet, anyhow."

"Well, slip down there every few minutes and keep me posted."

Libby faded silently into the stairwell.

"You can't send an eleven-year-old child down there to snitch," Margo said.

"She's big for her age."

"Henry!"

"A joke, Margo. For Heaven's sake."

"It wasn't funny."

"Nothing will happen to her."

Libby reappeared. "We've got two crashers."

"Bad?"

"Nah. Little guys. Thomas said it was okay."

"Are the linebackers in place?"

"Marty says he doesn't need them. Actually he couldn't get them."

"So that means we never had any security perimeter to begin with? That was supposed to be part of the contract."

Libby shrugged. She was an informer, not an enforcer.

By 11:30 the volume level from below had risen beyond the pain threshold. Henry had made two hasty visits to the basement and retreated in dismay. "You can't move down there. You can't see. You can't hear. Is that supposed to be fun?"

"Are there more than forty?"

"How does a hundred sound? Obviously we have no control beyond prayer at this point. I just hope we can close it down by three."

Libby had been sent to the master bedroom an hour ago, protesting vigorously. She reappeared now in the hallway. "What's happening?" she said.

"Go," said Henry. "Back to bed. Sleep."

"Ha," she said hollowly, in retreat.

A moment later Marty came up the stairs two at a time. "Henry," he said. "Could you come down and help me for a minute?"

It was the first time Marty had asked Henry for anything — almost the first time he'd addressed him by name. With mixed elation and apprehension, Henry followed him down the steps.

"What's going on?"

"Some of my unfriends came in. . . ." He said something more that was swallowed up in the tumult.

As though they had planned it, Henry flipped the light switch and Marty cut the sound within ten seconds of one another. The effect was like splitting an oak log in winter. A colony of woozy ants, disoriented in the glare, huddled together—except at the far end of the room where there was an explosion of four or five mad bodies snarling, fists swinging wildly, bodies out of control, perhaps twenty feet from where Henry stood. They seemed to be spilling out of Marty's room.

*"That's it!"* Henry roared. *"Hold it right there!"* No one had heard a sound like this come from Henry, ever. Everyone froze. The fighters began to slip out through the far door. Henry vaulted after them. *"Hey you! Where do you think you're going!"*

Outside there was the sound of running feet. An engine raced. Then there was silence.

"My fish!" A stricken cry from Marty's room. Several kids ran to see—Sandra, Libby, others. Henry followed.

In the room everything had been trashed. Drawers pulled and heaved, clothes strewn, bed upturned, chair splintered, all seen by the brazen glare of a swinging ceiling fixture—the only light left.

The tank was on its side, black against the floor. Water soaked the rug. One or two fish still flipped listlessly in the mess. Libby rushed out and came back with a pail of water and tried to scoop them up. She was crying.

"It's no use," Marty said quietly. "They have to have salt water." He put a hand on Libby's shoulder to comfort her.

The gesture—the tableau—stamped itself on Henry's mind, a strobe's print on the brain. Two boys were trying to reassemble the bed. Sandra and another girl were replacing the drawers, picking up sodden clothing and looking at it.

In the center stood Marty—upright, contained, almost uninvolved. He turned his head and for a few seconds his eyes and Henry's met, a look of such wordless intensity that Henry could remember it afterward only in terms of color—like jewels of refracted sunlight.

Two nights later Margo and Henry were watching the late news alone.

"Marty appreciated your help the other night," she told him without raising her head.

"I know."

"Oh? Did he actually speak to you about it?"

"Our communication is subliminal."

She smiled. "Well, at least it's communication. We seem to have to go to death's door to open up the channels, don't we? I passed along your offer to replace the fish, but he said he's outgrown them now."

"Ah, well . . ."

"Henry?"

"Yes, love?"

"You're a good father—for a Yankee."

"Is that a commendation or a reprimand?"

"But you're not much for hugging."

# 5

The whole idea of a family farm at Broad Run seemed frivolous for a Washington bureaucrat, except that it was the one thing all six of them shared. But there never was quite enough money or time to keep everything functioning properly. Barn roofs would leak, tractors would balk, roads would wash out, and the fences, the everlasting fences, would sag or break or die any of a thousand mysterious deaths, whether they were barbed-wire, mesh, or board, and the animals would escape—and the neighbors would call.

Often the call would come in the night and, like the occupants of a fire station, Henry and Margo and whichever children were home would leap into their clothes and run out into the darkness to bring the horses back before they headed for the highway or trampled Sam Newman's lawn. Sam was the most frequent caller.

Farming was not the center of Henry's life, or Margo's or of any of the children's lives, but none of them would have been willing to give it up. Even Marty, now away at school—briefly at one, then another—seemed to like to return home.

They tried raising everything but pigs—chickens, geese,

cattle, goats, sheep—but only the horses endured. Or perhaps the family could endure only the horses. This seemed self-indulgent to Henry, since horses provide man merely pleasure instead of vital necessities.

The truant herd was frequently led by Mischief, a pony-thoroughbred cross who had earned his name as a legendary comedian and magician. Fortunately for him, he was also the best children's eventing horse in Fauquier County or he'd have gone to the livestock sale ten times over.

Catching a horse that has a sense of humor is hard at best—impossible if the human does not have a sense of humor to match.

Thomas' fourteen-year-old sense of humor did not extend to loose horses. Everything was a test of strength. You could get him to work if there was a challenge to it—heaving bales of hay ten feet up into the loft, splitting heavy oak logs, carrying hundred-pound bags of feed. Even though he'd grown up on a farm, he believed he could outrun a horse and if necessary wrestle it to the ground. It was a fantasy belief, and it was all nonsense.

Margo and the girls knew this and would have preferred that Thomas stay in and watch TV, but if he sensed crisis nothing could deter him. He'd rush to the fields, the others trailing behind, hoping for something less than disaster.

One memorable night the horses got out in the middle of a deluge—one of those storms that starts out with a lot of thunder and lightning, then steadies to a downpour as though Somebody up there had got a good look at all the wenching and oral sex and pulled the big chain, and all the toilets in Heaven were being flushed on Fauquier County. It was September, a cool evening, windy and wet, and when they rushed out after the loose horses no one took time to dress carefully. Henry grabbed a waterproof storm jacket with a hood, and Margo and the girls each took some kind of poncho or light raincoat.

Thomas, the macho kid, led the brigade in shorts, tank top and muscles—and the Etonic running shoes Henry had just shelled out forty-five dollars for.

The horses didn't mind the rain. They were having a lovely time splashing around in it. In the dark it was hard to tell how many of them were out, but at a minimum it was Mischief and Snow Goose and two of the ponies.

On such nights everybody always wants a flashlight—for comfort, since they don't improve efficiency. If you use one to see the ground under your feet, your eyes never get accustomed to the dark, so you can't see anything else—certainly not a dark horse on a dark night in the rain. So you keep snapping it on and off to get a snapshot of that moving thing in the road that turns out to be one of the cats trying to divert you to the barn for an extra snack.

And of course flashlights were never where they belonged, which was in the trunk of each car, on the shelf of the hall closet, and on the right side of Henry's top bureau drawer. But no one put flashlights back—or replaced batteries—except Henry.

That night they found three flashlights: one under Thomas' bed, one in the kitchen drawer with the sharp knives, and one beneath the water heater in the laundry, where someone had used it to relight the pilot.

Thomas was using one of these precious three to hunt for the horses. Margo used the second to hunt for the hunters, and Henry took the third. He intended to use it to find the side gap if somebody caught a horse.

This gap was a break in the fence, bridged by a handmade net of barbed wire and pieces of tree branch, wired in place with more barbed wire. It had to serve as an emergency entrance and to be horse-proof, which meant it was hard for a human to open, even in the daylight, without getting stuck. To try it at night without a flashlight would have been hopeless. Even with a light it was hard, because you had to use two hands. If somebody was yelling at you and you were soaking wet, you could count on cutting yourself at least twice.

By the time Henry got out to the barn he could hear Margo and Libby and Sandra and Thomas all yelling.

"Don't *run* to him, you idiot!" This was Margo.

"I didn't, Mom!"

"You did too! I saw you!" Libby never missed a chance to make Thomas look bad.

"Shut up, Libby!" (How many times had Henry heard this?)

"Here," said Sandra, "if you have to be the hero, take this bucket of corn and walk up to him slowly. Shake it so he can hear what you've got."

"I can't shake it! It's all wet!"

"Put pebbles in it. They'll rattle," called Margo.

"But he can't eat pebbles!"

"Just do it! Just so he hears it!"

"But that's a dirty trick to put in pebbles. He'll never trust me again!"

"Thomas—for God's sake!"

"I've got Snow Goose! I've got Snow Goose!" Sandra had sensibly sneaked up on the white mare, visible even in the dark. "Somebody bring me a lead shank. She hasn't got a halter. All I've got hold of is her mane. . . . No, Thomas! No, Thomas! You dumb shit! I'm going inside. You're the stupidest shit in the whole world!"

"What happened? What happened?" Four voices called out, including Henry's. Nobody could see anything except the intermittent pinprick of a flashlight now and then. The rain was making so much noise that no one could hear anyone else. Everyone was soaked through. Water was pouring from Henry's scalp. His glasses were hopeless. He took refuge in the barn with the excuse of looking for lead shanks. But Margo and Libby had all the lead shanks. Outside, just beyond the fence, Henry could hear the sound of pounding hooves as the horses galloped happily up and down.

"Henry! Open the gap! Maybe we can drive them in!"

"I almost got trampled!"

"Well, get out of the way, stupid!"

Sandra held the flashlight while Henry gingerly unhooked the tendrils of barbed wire and pulled the apparatus from the gap.

"Hold the light so we can see it! You, Thomas, get over there! Libby to my right! Sandra, where the hell are you!" Margo bludgeoned them into concert of action if not spirit, and after three tries the horses were finally herded home. Actually, Mischief was tired of the game and decided to go for the run-in shed where he might find something to eat, and the others followed. Then the animals of higher intelligence straggled back to the house grousing at one another, Margo in the middle of it because she loved it, Henry hanging back because he hated it.

By the time he got to the kitchen, the three women and Thomas had assumed roles of picadors and bull, with Thomas already charging blindly at his adversaries, who knew with great precision where to lance, how to enrage.

He was an easy target. All his faults and virtues were wonderfully conspicuous. Beautiful in body, slovenly in living habits, by turn sweet-natured and churlish, arrogant, sensitive to point of pain, this adolescent boy guarded his sisters' honor like a medieval knight and bullied them like a straw boss. One of his games to drive them crazy was walking in on them when they were watching TV and changing the program. It instantly transformed Libby into a witch.

Tonight after his loose horses performance the females were adjusting the accounts with no male to interfere. Marty wasn't home, and Henry, shameful coward, exited to his library and tried not to listen, telling himself that Thomas had earned every penny of it. There was no need to hear what the women were saying, but Thomas' roars penetrated the walls: "Shut up, Libby! Shut up, Sandra! Shut up, Mom!"

There followed a series of crashes that could no longer be ignored. Henry raced to the kitchen to find Thomas doing his best to punch out the wall cabinets with bare knuckles because a thousand years of chivalry forbade him to knock down a woman. He would have ruined either the cabinets or his fists if Henry hadn't intervened with a glancing blow to the shoulder and by bellowing his name.

Thomas swung around, bloody-eyed. Here was somebody he could maim—a stepfather. "You wanna have it out! Come outside!"

Henry backed away, trying to maintain some dignity in the face of such fury, saying "Simmer down," or something equally useful. Suddenly Thomas turned and bolted from the room. "I hate you!" he screamed, voice breaking, heart breaking. "I hate all of you!" The front door slammed. "You'll never see me again!" he howled, heading out into the rain and darkness toward the back fields.

In the shuddering silence that followed, the expressions Henry saw ranged from rue to amusement to indignation. Libby, ever the tally chief, inspected the cupboard doors for damage. "Someday he's going to kill somebody," she said.

"At least it wasn't you he hit," Henry said.

"He hits us," Sandra said.

63

"Not hard, though."

"Hard enough."

"Shouldn't I go after him?"

"No!" said both girls at once. "He's just crazy."

"In a little while, maybe," Margo said.

"I think you all go crazy. You drive each other crazy," Henry told them.

Sandra turned to her favorite anesthetic: *Love Boat* was on.

When Henry finally stepped outside, the ground under his feet felt like the plastic sponge from the kitchen sink. The rain had stopped, leaving wet silence behind. No breeze, no geese wheeling overhead, not even dogs barking. One cat tried cleaving to his calf but gave up and returned to the woodshed where it was dry.

At least it wasn't cold.

He walked a hundred yards back from the house toward the barn, cupped his hands, and called Thomas' name. If he wouldn't come in yet, he could at least know the family wanted him. Sometimes you wondered if he wanted himself. Only the scrimmage line or the weight room could contain such a spirit.

Henry called over and over, walking almost half a mile, into the farthest pasture, before he gave up. We love you, Thomas—come back and try again.

Not those words, of course. Only his name, two syllables, two notes into the darkness.

When Henry and Margo finally went to bed they left the outside lights on and a lamp burning in the living room. Henry lay back, knowing sleep wouldn't come until they heard the front door slam. With Thomas, doors always slammed.

But not this night. He materialized silently beside the bed. "Mom, could you come and help me for a minute?"

Margo went with him to the kitchen, came back to the

bathroom medicine cabinet, returned to the kitchen. Henry could hear voices, but only faintly. At least he was in safe hands now. Henry dozed.

When she came back and slipped into his arms he could feel her suppressing something.

"What?"

"He got caught in barbed wire. He ran into it at twenty-five miles an hour, he said. He's got about fifteen little cuts and two sort of bad ones. He took it as a sign God wanted him to come home and try harder."

Henry wrote a ballad that was posted for the winter on the side of the refrigerator. The first stanza began:

Thomas and Libby were flint and steel,
They made hot sparks at the evening meal,
Then Mom looked worried and Dad wore a frown
And the dog slunk away and the air turned brown.

The final stanza concluded that they fought because they loved one another. Whenever this part was read they would exchange a look and pretend to vomit.

Thomas had been ten when Henry married Margo, and Libby, eight. Their strange interdependence and epic quarreling struck Henry as symbolic of the struggle each of them felt as they strove to make a whole family from the two fragmented ones, from rhythms as different as the moon and a volcano.

Sandra referred to the Thomas-and-Libby relationship as the Ten Years' War, but it seemed to Henry that there were times when the term applied to all of them.

Sometimes the farm really did work almost like the dream, when the timothy and clover in June grew thick as a woman's hair, then was cut for three days' drying time with fingers crossed against the thunderstorms. And the fourth morning would start with an undercurrent of carnival excitement when Henry on the '53 blue Ford Jubilee pulled a flatbed wagon with kids all over it, Henry's four and four more, and Margo perched up against the tractor's fender with an arm across Henry's shoulders, across two middle pastures, through a fringe of hardwoods, emerging finally onto the thirty-three-acre hay-field in brassy sunlight where Sam Newman in his cowboy hat would already have started baling, perched on his '72 International Harvester with the baler snatching up the windrows, huffing, chunking, and spitting out bales of aromatic grasses as square as a Marine's crew cut. And half the crew would hook another flatbed to the baler to catch and stack them as they came, and the rest would stack from the ground as Henry pulled through them, yelling, laughing, quarreling as always, piling them six rows high, so they tilted like skyscrapers in an earthquake with every turn of the wagon's wheel, as the second crew inched back to the barn to throw the bales up to the loft (Thomas shining and hollering) to Libby and Sandra and Henry who slid them across the smooth-worn, pumpkin-colored boards and stacked them in the hot loft's gloom, emerging again and again for a breath of air and a gulp of lemonade—back and forth, load after load in the loft's 115-degree heat until at four in the afternoon there were twelve hundred bales massed to the rafters and the whole loft smelled like lentil soup, and everyone itched and poured sweat until they fell one after another into the horse-pond at the dam, and that tepid muddy water felt like loving to the skin.

There were other days and nights . . . baby-sitting a foaling mare, cold April nights, taking turns at the sleeping bag in the barn until the miraculous blue delivery . . . battling back-to-back blizzards with shovels and tractors and plows and neighbors' plows, breath bright-gleaming in a morning-after landscape of white drifts and cedar green and the soft-laden pines down the long driveway . . . hand-scavenging November corn after the machine had passed . . . felling the final elms with chain saws, then trying to exorcise the damned things, each one exploding on the splitter's blade as its demon was driven from the grain—and all this with adolescent zeal and snarl and cachinnation and discombobulation, because nothing was ever low-key.

Each one of them had a private chain saw chewing away inside, the girls perhaps even more than the boys, certainly no one more than Sandra, for whom getting up in the morning and brushing her teeth was a prelude to high drama, who experienced religious conversion not once but sequentially, who was top achiever with least natural ability, literal-minded, loving, shamelessly greedy, possessed of a voice that could croon a puppy to sleep or split a solid oak chopping block.

Margo's children were all noisy, but Sandra had a special piercing quality. She had more raw courage than either of her brothers, but everything she did made noise—laughing, crying, running up a flight of stairs, sewing on a button. She was the one who consistently brought home A's from school. She could stick on a horse like a monkey. She had a mouth that got her in trouble at one time or another with everyone she knew.

As a little girl Sandra had been a doll. Margo could dress her, could teach her to ride, could play games of make-believe with her, count on her to be helpful in house and barn, tell the truth, live up to her promises. Sandra was fun, as responsive and lively as her mother. Until she hit adolescence she looked like a gerbil.

Sometime between eleven and fourteen the joy had slipped away, as Sandra became a succession of new selves, each more horrifying than the one just past. The first overt signs were frightful applications of eye makeup, a variety of exotic, failed hair experiments, and breasts.

Her downstairs room, never tidy, became a welter of clothes that lay where they fell, along with damp towels, dirty dishes, half-eaten food, records without jackets. From this room came the rock music that made the floors vibrate under Margo's feet, even through the soles of her barn boots.

This was standard adolescent fare, so she could accept it as a normal phase. A door could be closed upon it (except the stereo, which she handled by removing the fuses from the circuits to Sandra's room once or twice a week as required).

What made her flesh crawl was Sandra's personal hygiene. The boys showered their gleaming bodies for hours on end. Sandra put off bathing and snapped back if pushed about it. Her outer clothes looked decent because it was Margo who washed and ironed them and handed them to her. But she would wear her underclothes for days until they were gray. Her hair was washed once a week if Margo hounded her. Her disposal of pads and tampons was the subject of secret, hissing mother-daughter guerrilla warfare.

In house, barn, and kitchen she became a liability. It was Sandra, for instance, who showed Thomas how to cook a cheese hot dog without a pan, by placing it directly on the gas burner. . . .

When Margo would erupt into volcanic wrath over a series of these atrocities, Sandra would respond by pointing out Margo's own hypocrisies and inconsistencies.

"You've wrecked my life!"

It took Margo's breath away. "You're not even born yet. What life?"

"You did! You've stunted my emotional development."

"Where did you even hear such language? I'll stunt you. I'll make you do all the dishes for a week for your big mouth. How did I stunt you?"

"You wouldn't let me get my ears pierced."

"When you're eighteen you can pierce anything you want. How about your nose?"

"You see! You don't take me seriously. I'm a sensitive human being."

"I'll take you seriously when you rinse your dishes and put them in the washer, when you flush the toilet after yourself, when you change your underpants every morning."

"Mother!" Sandra rolled her eyes toward Thomas watching TV.

"If you've got bad habits, clean 'em up."

"I hate you! You love to humiliate me! You're trying to destroy me!" This was accompanied by high-volume weeping, tortured body and facial language.

"Shut up, Sandra. I can't even hear the gunfire."

But Thomas' complaint would be lost in the melee of screaming and slamming that ensued for fifteen full minutes, upstairs and down, with Margo in a hypercharged state if not tears and Sandra racked by great heaving, histrionic sobbing spasms. They would separate for two minutes to breathe, whereupon the upstairs person would go down to mount a new offensive (falsely labeled as a peace initiative) for another ten minutes of screaming. Counting the break time, the combat could continue for as long as two hours, leaving the contestants and everyone within earshot exhausted.

The final outcome would usually be the escape of Henry and Thomas, to return much later with the pizza that was eaten by everyone (including Sandra) in sepulchral silence from which all emotion had been drained.

When Sandra had spilled out all the family's dark secrets, from Marty's felony record to Thomas' bowel habits, she had expected Henry would be equally open with her. She accepted his divorce from Libby's adoptive mother, but she demanded a full explanation, including disclosure of sexual compatibility or insufficiency thereof. It never occurred to her that Henry would be less than fully candid. When she finally discovered that Henry had been married *twice* before, she was hurt.

"You never said one word about it," she said accusingly.

"I'm sorry, sweetie. I have trouble just dumping these things out for display."

"No wonder Libby wants to keep everything a secret. She's copying you. Don't call me sweetie when I'm mad at you. I want to know everything about her."

"Well, her name was Ruthless Carver and we fought all the time." Henry stopped.

"Really? Ruthless?"

"No. Really Ruth. But she was ruthless."

"Well, what else?"

"What else did you want to know?"

"Everything. Where did you meet her? How long were you married? Was she pretty? Was she cheating on you? Where is she now?"

"In college, twelve years, no, yes, and I haven't any idea."

Sandra's eyes filled with tears. "You're being mean!"

He was being mean and niggardly. Old pain was almost impossible to share. Yet here sat this adoring, stormy child demanding his secrets in return for her own. If you love me give me of yourself.

So bit by bit Henry tried to relate the story of a love battered and long dead as he and Sandra sat by a poor fire on a Sunday afternoon in November. As he talked Henry kept poking at the logs, but they hissed and refused to blaze.

Ruth had hissed through her teeth at him—a cute-angry game. Amusing for a while. She had been a Carver and could trace her ancestry back to the *Mayflower*'s second voyage. Henry's mother had loved it. But Ruth had hated her own unattractive body, so the world had to suffer her rage. She was angular and she was pockmarked by childhood acne.

"How could you marry someone like that?"

"She was the only one in school smarter than I was."

"You don't marry for that."

"I did. I fell in love with her brain. She also loved to take men to bed."

Sandra's eyes widened. This was more like it.

But it was a perverse love, a grasping love, a love that consumed men like grapes.

"Did you sleep with her before you were married?"

"Sandra, I was twenty-two years old, a veteran home from Germany."

"I guess that means yes, huh?"

Sandra had to find out for herself. Even pain sounded exciting if it came from hopeless romance, and no adult was going to tell her differently. Whether it was coincidence or an unconscious imitation of what she conceived as Henry's dramatic early marriage, Sandra's first serious boyfriend was angular and pockmarked and not only sullen but cruel, judging from the tortures Sandra seemed to suffer.

His name was Vance Mountcastle, which alone was enough to set Henry's teeth on edge. His second offense was owning a Harley-Davidson Low Rider. Supported by a rare unanimous family vote, Henry decreed the motorcycle off-limits, to Sandra's annoyance. She pointed out that she was practically seventeen.

This year also saw one of the several climaxes in Sandra's divorce action from her mother with its alternating periods of rage and quiet, deep confidences. Henry's role was usually that of mediator—not in the traditional go-between fashion (which would have been impossible with two screaming maniacs who upset him equally) but simply by being available. Once he told Sandra that if she was ever stuck anywhere, at any hour, he would come and get her with no questions asked.

And Henry listened. The rest of the family would have said he talked as much as anyone, but mostly he listened.

The year of Vance Mountcastle was a terrible year for everyone, and for none more than Sandra, who was ready to die for him. Perhaps it was a terrible year for Sandra's whole class. Word came of one boy who had shot himself over a lost love, and of another girl who, at fourteen, had run away with a twenty-two-year-old drag racer to Mississippi when her parents forbade her to see him and swore out a warrant for his arrest if he should come again to visit. Marty and Thomas thought it was ridiculous. Sandra and Libby voiced no opinion, which Henry took to mean they were envious. He convinced Margo they would best let Sandra have at her animal and try to ride it out.

It wasn't an easy decision. There were continued debates about the wisdom of it as Sandra trudged through her days and wept through her nights, confiding in no one, her candor gone.

There would be phone calls on weeknights, imperious sum-

PAUL ESTAVER

monses on the weekends. Sandra responded to them all with the light of love in her eyes and concluded them all with tears of rage. Once she descended to her bedroom and smashed all her mirrors in a solitary tantrum that left the rest of the house in stunned silence.

When Margo looked stricken Henry shook his head. "So long as she's keeping school hours and getting in by eleven on Friday and Saturday nights, we've got to let her work it out."

"That boy will destroy her, Henry."

"Nobody's going to destroy Sandra Bishop. Evidently you haven't noticed her strong instinct for self-preservation."

"You pick strange times to try being funny."

"I'm not being funny. I'm deadly serious."

"I'm telling you, if a bunch of motorcycle freaks get their hands on her she could wind up gang-raped or dead."

"And I'm telling you, Sandra isn't going to let it happen. Vance isn't in a motorcycle gang. His father owns that Mountcastle Hardware there across from the fire station."

It didn't prove anything to Margo. She continued to fume. The longer it dragged on, the less sure Henry became of his own wisdom. Maybe it would be best just to kick the boy out, tell her he was banished. *But then we lose her confidence. She can't go on like this. Give it two more weeks.* They watched the clock as Sandra groped through the fall.

When the end did come, it was closer to a disaster than Henry had allowed himself to predict. There was a 2:00 a.m. phone call on a Saturday night when Sandra was supposedly staying at a girlfriend's house.

"Did you mean it—about coming to get me with no questions asked?" A frightened child's voice in the darkness.

"Where are you?"

"Rose's Motel." The hot pillow palace where the rednecks went to burn up the weekends.

73

"I'll be right there."

It was December—an ice-cold, windy night expressed in from Saskatchewan. Fifteen minutes later when Henry pulled into the motel driveway there was no one in sight. Then suddenly she was jumping into he seat beside him, slamming the door, hissing, "Go! Quick! Hurry!"

Henry hurried. Sandra became a ball of rags in the corner. He couldn't tell whether she was sobbing. Her coat was someone else's, a man's, much too big.

"Would you like me to ride around a little bit?" he said.

"No."

"Anything else I can do? Physical violence? Break a few fingers?"

"No. Just go home."

He drove on, not fast.

"I'm never going to see him again!" she said. "I hope you and Mom are satisfied!"

"Whoa, baby. We never said a word."

"You didn't have to."

"In this country you don't hang for what you think."

But he asked no questions and she volunteered no explanations. She bolted past Margo down to her room as soon as they entered the house. When Margo moved to follow he put a hand on her arm. "We promised no questions."

She paused on the top step, staring up at him. "Okay," she said finally. "No questions. But I can't not go to her. She's my daughter, Henry."

It was almost five before Margo came up. Henry had been dozing fitfully, not quite dreaming but somehow watching a theater screen filled with menacing figures that he could never quite control nor escape. Once he thought he heard Sandra cry out and sat up fully awake, then tiptoed down into the basement stairwell until he could hear women's voices, like doves in a grove of pine trees.

When she did come up Margo settled into bed still in her robe, looking pale and exhausted. "Close call," she said, "but I think we passed a milestone."

Henry waited while Margo lay propped on her pillows staring at the far wall, smoking absently. Finally he said, "I've been lying here doubting everything I know. How bad was it?"

"I'm not to tell you details. She doesn't want you to think she's a fallen person, she said."

"How bad was it?"

She smiled a little and patted his leg through the bedclothes. "It's so hard to tell when you care sometimes. It's gratifying to know you do, a little."

"I care a lot," he said crossly. "How bad was it?"

"Apparently he took her and another girl to the motel and wanted to take both of them to bed. When Sandra wouldn't he started making love to the other girl while Sandra stood there. She'd had too much to drink. He was counting on that to keep her there—thinking she'd be scared to call you."

Henry drew a deep breath. "Do you think they'd had sex before?"

"Where's your permissiveness now?"

"It's not even a matter of permissiveness. I just don't think you can put a child in prison. Not these days." He rolled over and closed his eyes.

Margo turned out the light and put her arms around him. "It's okay, darling. You were great. She's through with it now.

We spent a long time talking about love and God. She's going back to her super-church."

Henry thought about it for a few minutes. Then just as Margo's breathing became slow and regular, he said, "Have you ever noticed that our little flock of Episcopalians are either prepubescent or postmenopausal?"

"What? Why are you still talking?"

"We have no young adults. As soon as they become sexually active they have to abandon us. We don't even have confession to let them off the hook. So they go to the charismatics to get forgiven and sing in four-part harmony."

"Go to sleep, Henry."

The room was silent except for the quiet rush of air from the heating vents. Henry's eyes became heavy.

"Henry?"

"Yes?"

"She loves you. She said to thank you."


Sandra's rebirth was more trying to Margo than for Henry because Margo cared about God. Sandra announced that she was forgiven, with the clear implication that the rest of the family were not. She spoke of herself as a Christian. She sang a lot.

Margo tolerated it better before she realized Sandra had acquired a new tactical weapon in the Scriptures. She would follow her mother around the house pointing the finger of condemnation.

"Jesus Christ, Sandra! This is the third time you've left the feed-room door open. Are you deliberately trying to kill the horses!"

"Thou shalt not take the name of the Lord thy God in vain."

It didn't stop there, either. In one daring feint Sandra made a less-than-oblique reference to the fact that Margo and Henry had disappeared overnight before their wedding had taken place.

"How do you think we felt, huddled at home with an adulteress for a mother roaming in the night?"

"Goddammit, Sandra, I wasn't exactly a scarlet woman."

"Thou shalt not . . ."

The denouement—or at least the conclusion—of Sandra's holy period occurred in conjunction with the prayer meetings she held in the rec room.

Henry noticed that not all the participants departed when the singing ended. "Do you think we should be chaperoning them?"

"Do you think we really need to?"

"That huge one seems to be staying the night."

"I'm sure he's on the couch. He's very sweet."

"Is he the former Hell's Angel?"

"Sandra says he's God's angel now."

"How much do you believe that on a scale of ten?" This conversation took place in the master bedroom at approximately two o'clock on a Wednesday morning. Henry and Margo had just made very quiet love. Sandra was within two months of graduating from high school.

"I think you're ducking the issue," said Henry. Margo could feel him grinning into the dark.

"Wouldn't it look a bit hypocritical going down in the gown of purity? After all, I've been branded an adulteress."

"You don't have to avenge. Just go chat with them. Sit there and have a cigarette. Wait him out."

Margo put her arms around him. "You go, Henry."

"She's your daughter."

"You shit! I don't ask very much of you. Besides, she loves you."

With a sigh Henry rose and began to put on a sweat suit, but in the end it was Margo who went, smoked endless cigarettes, outlasted Sandra's giant, then engaged in an emotional wrestling match with Sandra that rent the darkness for another hour. Henry was reading when she crawled back into bed.

"You're awake!"

"How could I be otherwise?"

"I thought we were quiet."

"Only by comparison to Washington National Airport."

"She says she's leaving home."

"Do you think we could bribe her to stay with the offer of a free college education?"

"Be serious. She's impossible, Henry. She tells me I'm losing my mind. She says I'm selfish and unfeeling—and crazy. Do I seem crazy to you?"

"Just when you're mothering Sandra."

Sandra didn't leave until the fall semester at Randolph-Macon began. But her visits home were never easy. She and Margo had trouble getting through a single day in peace. The passing of Sandra's charismatic period made her less hypocritical but not more forgiving. Margo despaired.

"You try and try," she told Henry. "You read the right books, you take them to church, you give them your energy and love and strength. You share your beliefs with them. And then they turn out to be monsters. Marty's a zombie, Thomas is so in love with himself he kisses the mirrors, and Sandra's a harpy."

"Aren't you a little harsh?"

"I have to be, to beat you to the gun."

Henry only shook his head.

"You know what she's into now?"

"Let me guess—heroin?"

"That's the trouble with you. One minute you're sitting in judgment there—"

"How?"

"—without uttering a word. With just your eyebrows. And the next minute you won't take it seriously."

"I get upset with the little things and laugh at the big ones."

"How about marijuana—big or little?"

Margo had found out about the marijuana the same way she learned everything else about Sandra. Sandra had told her. She had never lied to protect herself as the others did because she was never afraid of what would happen. She was happy to fight about it. In a cage, she tested every bar.

There were times when Margo would rather have been spared the details, but this was not Sandra's game. If the subject of masturbation arose you heard all about when Sandra did it, under what circumstances, how often, originating at what point in her life. If it made anyone squirm, so much the better.

Thus Margo came to know about all whom Sandra fell in love and slept with. She never went to bed with anyone she didn't love, but she loved quite a few, including a VMI cadet, a law student at UVA, a summer lifeguard, two of her teachers, one clergyman, and, briefly, a housemother.

"Shouldn't we report it?" Margo wondered about the last.

"Why?" said Henry. "It's not a disease. Besides, you can't betray Sandra's confidence."

"All this confidence is scrambling my brain. I'm not equipped to deal with the new morality."

"Is it so different from the old?"

"I wasn't like that. I never slept with anyone until I was married."

"But you kissed them and they patted your ass and touched you—as they still did when I met you and you drove me up the wall."

"I've told you—it didn't mean anything."

"It doesn't matter any more."

# 6

---•◆•---

"You're going to New Hampshire for how long?" Margo was half-listening, trying to watch the news and get supper at the same time.

"Wednesday through Friday. Then I want to go look at Lake Winnipesaukee for the weekend. I want you to come with me."

"Oh, honey, I can't. We've already got two big training groups in and a wedding group Saturday."

"Get someone else to work for you."

"I can't. We're already short two. There's only Kit and me left."

With the farm work, her job and his, the forty-mile commute from Broad Run to Washington, and the school events with mandatory parental participation, Henry and Margo were lucky to find time for a movie once a month.

"Tell me again what you're doing up there."

"It's a training seminar for community mediators at the university conference center in Durham. Then I'll go look at the lake."

Margo shivered. "It's too cold up there in April."

"It'll be May."

"But only just barely. You go by yourself if you want."

"You want me up there alone?"

She looked at him sharply. "What are you going to do—pick up a cookie?"

Henry blew a puff of air through his nostrils as Yankees do when they laugh. "Hardly," he said; then, abruptly aware that his exotic new Japanese-American secretary was scheduled to be conference registrar, he took Margo in his arms. "I never want to do anything to hurt you," he said.

Suki Senda's part in the conference was legitimate. She was one of four office staffers to attend. There was more than enough to keep her busy. Henry had not mentioned her to Margo because he seldom talked about the office at home. The only thing he did that he might not have done with Margo along was offer Suki a ride to the airport. She lived in Arlington, barely out of his way.

At 5:15 on the Wednesday morning when he knocked at her door she greeted him dressed and ready.

"You're early," she said.

"It's a disease."

"We must be very quiet. Everyone else is asleep. Sit down. Coffee?"

He shook his head, and she disappeared somewhere out back. The living room was tiny, like its occupant. The furniture was sparse, simple. It felt oriental even though it was domestic stuff: two chairs, a coffee table, a low settee. On the walls were two photographs mounted on woodblocks. One was very Japanese: a close-up of drops of dew on a spider web in what appeared to be silvery early-morning light. The dewdrops and a few strands of the web were in razor-sharp focus. Everything else was lost in haze, with just a hint of a pastel color spectrum.

The other photo was a black and white of an old lady sitting on a bench at the edge of a beach. It was obviously a warm day, but she was fully dressed in black, seen from behind, wearing a ridiculous floppy black hat. Her clothing, her hat, and the mid-morning stark shadows all combined to portray a turkey buzzard. And in the distance, at the ocean's edge, were a young man and woman in bathing suits, romping with a ball in the brilliant sunlight.

Henry became so lost in these—particularly the second picture—that he hardly heard Suki reenter the room.

"What a strange picture for a young woman to have on her wall," he said.

"You like it?"

"I don't know if liking is the right word. It disturbs me. It's painful. Why do you have such a thing in your living room?"

"It's one of my best. It won me a couple of prizes."

"You do these things?"

"Oh yes. But I don't process my color stuff."

"But you print the rest? Where?"

"Out back." She waved a hand. "Should we go? It's after half past." She pulled on a jacket and picked up a substantial suitcase, leading the way out. Henry followed, enjoying his own amazement. Because she was so tiny he'd tended to see her as a child. The self-possession now was startling. A Western person, he thought, couldn't look at once so understated and so dramatic. Her skin was ivory, her hair like a black teardrop about her head. As far as Henry could tell her only makeup might have been something about the eyes, but her face was etched in the dawn light.

At Washington National she politely refused Henry's offer to drop her at the terminal and rode with him to the parking area. "I often walk this time of day," she said. "To watch the sun rise—when it's not too hazy." She spoke the unaccented English of the West Coast, but her phrasing felt oriental to him.

"I won't be able to take you home. I'm staying in New

Hampshire until Sunday afternoon," he told her as they walked toward the terminal.

"Oh? Old friends?"

"No, I have a brother there, but I won't see him this time. There's a big lake called Winnipesaukee that means 'smile of the great spirit,' where I went summers when I was a young man. I'm going to go and look at it for two days."

There was a long silence. Finally Suki asked if his lake was very beautiful.

"Yes," he said. "Very beautiful. I'm going alone to lose myself in it for a little while—an escape from voices."

Another long silence. They approached the terminal and asked for their gate. Too early yet.

"Coffee?" asked Henry.

"No, thank you. But you go."

"Come keep me company."

"You wouldn't mind?"

"Of course not. What a strange question."

"But you like to be alone. To lose yourself."

"Not at Washington National Airport."

She was still again as he bought coffee and carried it to the table, sat, dumped a creamer into it.

"I've never seen New Hampshire," she said when he glanced at her. "Is all of it very beautiful?"

"Parts of it are nice. We'll pass some water on our way to Durham."

"I have my camera. Perhaps I could get pictures of this water?"

Henry peered at her over his glasses. It occurred to him that she might be persuaded to stay for the weekend. He could do it fairly safely. He could get her a room of her own so that it would be innocent if not credible. In any case Margo needn't know.

No, he decided. Too risky. With the purest of intentions, too risky. He didn't need a girlfriend. He certainly couldn't appear to be playing dirty-old-man games. Definitely no.

"How will I get back to Boston?" she said abruptly.

Henry drained the last of the coffee. "Suki," he said, "if I could arrange for separate living accommodations for you, would you like to go see my lake?"

She hadn't expected it. She held her breath for a moment, suppressing a smile. "If I go," she said, "I would promise to leave you completely alone. I would take my camera and explore by myself."

They would have to change her flight to Sunday, Henry thought, and somehow be sure the other two office staffers wouldn't notice. They'd flown up ahead and would leave promptly. But Suki in her innocence might say the wrong thing. When he looked at her it was as though his train of thought had been visible above his head.

"I would be very discreet," she said quietly.

At the Moon Palace Henry ate a solitary breakfast, enjoying the view of Lake Winnipesaukee dotted with furry islands, stretching out for some twenty miles from the motel on its headland above Weirs Beach. He found himself wishing that Suki were less literal-minded. If she was going to hang around for the weekend it seemed the least she could do was hang where she could be seen. He had risen at seven and found her neither in her room nor anywhere else in the vicinity. Then he remembered he'd told her not to disturb him before eight.

The ride up Friday evening had been for Henry a reunion with the rough-cut landscape of New Hampshire. From Durham he'd driven west on Route 4 toward Northwood, then north on 125 toward Rochester, roads unchanged in the twenty years since he'd seen them.

"This used to be a railroad," he told Suki. "Otherwise it would never be so straight. It's called the Calef Highway."

"Your family name!"

"Yes, but we don't know the Calefs up here. I'm from Massachusetts. There's a Calef's Store coming up. I went in to see them once and we guessed we must be third cousins."

"That could never happen to a Japanese family. Families are too important to lose. I know all my relatives."

"How many is that?"

"Hundreds, I guess. I never counted."

From Rochester northward Henry became confused by new construction as they drove. "This doesn't look right," he kept saying. But then on the long slope down toward Alton Bay and with his first glimpse of blue water through the trees he felt his childhood excitement again, his emotional clock turned back forty years to a boy's love of the land and its trees and water—and the sounds of wind through shoreline birch trees, of waves lapping shores, slapping pilings, of spring's peepers scoring the music of the opening of the land to the sun-warmed days. Three times as they followed the ancient roller-coaster road along the shoreline Henry had to stop and stand outside the car to smell the black-earth odors of spring and feel the cold air against his face.

"I keep seeing the child in you," Suki said laughing. Her delight in everything around her was so infectious that it became part of Henry's renewal. Nothing she said was provocative, but everything she did told him she loved being with him and assumed his feelings about Lake Winnipesaukee were part of his feelings for her.

He tried to remember to feel guilty without much success.

He was too peaceful. Last night there had been a bit of discomfort when he and Suki had presented themselves to the bear at the registration desk.

"We want two rooms," Henry said.

"You want what!" said the bear.

"Two rooms!" said Henry.

The bear looked at him in disgust.

"I'm her chauffeur," said Henry.

"And I'm Raquel Welch," said the bear, handing them two keys. "Enjoy your night."

Henry sat now in a corner of the dining room by a wall of windows overlooking the vista down past a scattering of guest houses, down the slope to the lake, cerulean blue in the cold spring light. Still early in the season for boats—only one cruiser visible in the miles of expanse. A view almost gone to waste. He was the sole customer on an eight o'clock Saturday morning. The waitress had dumped his pancakes before him and gone away to lurk in the shadows.

Then Suki was with him, vibrant as a bird just in from the south. She laid the back of an icy hand against his cheek, removed the bulky camera and equipment bag from around her neck and put them carefully on an extra chair. Then she sat down and smiled. She was wearing a jacket and turtleneck—and a pair of blue jeans three sizes too large, rolled up at the ankles.

"Cold cold," she said. "But so fresh. The air is like a flower petal this morning. Wonderful! May I steal some coffee from your pot?"

"Where did you get those pants?" said Henry. "Where have you been?" It was impossible not to respond to the gaiety.

"I bought them from Roy for six dollars. . . . I couldn't go out in my good skirt to climb fences and walk through fields. I've been out taking pictures of the lake—and, oh, a foal dancing in a pasture. His mother was very disapproving. Oh, Henry, you must come and see him." The smell of spring drifted to him from her hair and clothing. He found himself wanting to go and see a foal with her.

"Who's Roy?" he said.

"A funny little bellman at the desk."

"Obviously not as little as you," Henry said drily.

They sat quietly enjoying May and the lake below. She had long since eaten, she told him.

"Henry," she said after a few minutes. "I want you to tell me the truth."

He smiled and waited.

"Would you rather be alone? Do you want me to go away? I can enjoy myself exploring and meet you tonight, but if you'd like to enjoy with me I could—" She stopped anxiously. "I don't want to impose. I can't tell what goes on inside your head. It's very dark in there."

"I'd like us to share today," he told her. "Tomorrow we'll have to start back in the morning."

They moved out to the rental car and headed up through Meredith and around the north side of the lake, stopping by each inlet that gleamed in the sunlight. The freshness of cool air, the sun now warm, the smell of the earth all combined to fix the morning under glass as though past and future had vaporized and the only reality was now.

"Have you read *Shogun?*" he asked. They were sitting on a dock at Center Harbor looking down through six feet of black water at the sandy bottom. He could almost taste the air. The scent of pine woodsmoke drifted from a nearby cottage at the water's edge. Two crows flapped and cawed above the trees.

"No, but I have heard of it. It's about medieval Japan."

"Yes. This morning is like something from *Shogun*—its

stillness, its unreal quality. In the book they speak of things like watching stones grow and drinking tea from an empty cup. Cha, it's called."

"Yes, I know cha."

"I couldn't understand those things at first. I think I do better today."

"Yes." She seemed almost to be speaking from the book, small and deferential beside him, propped up against a piling on the dock.

"And the presence everywhere of death. And the preciousness of life. Of a dawn—a gift of a dawn it spoke of. Is Japanese life still the way that was?"

"Maybe in some ways. I've only visited." She placed her hand lovingly on her camera. "This is my attempt to make life precious."

"It looks expensive."

"It is. It's a Nikon. My father gave it to me. . . . May I take your picture?"

"Me? Why?"

"You have a beautiful head. A beautiful face."

"That's ridiculous. I'm not a good-looking man."

"Not good-looking. Beautiful. You are like a horse."

"Horse-faced, you mean."

She giggled. "Horses are beautiful," she said and stood up to find the proper angle for him.

By mid-afternoon they had worked their way down to Wolfeboro, across to Alton Bay again, and back to Glendale, Suki shooting, then sharing the camera with him. Several times he used her as a model after they had worked out a composition and she had calculated the settings. And she continued to shoot him when he was unaware of her. It made him uncomfortable to hear words like graceful applied to himself. She told him the discomfort was Western and appropriate, but she didn't stop using the terms.

"Oh, I love you," she said once as she watched him move easily over the rocks.

"So to speak," he said.

"I mean I love what you are. I mean you delight me. I mean, 'You have given me something.' I do not mean, 'You must give me something.'"

"Under that definition I could say I love you."

"Under that definition it is easy to love. I love many people."

"Even with the difference in ages?"

"What difference does age make?"


When the sun dropped behind the Belknap Range, the air turned cold. They drove back to the Moon Palace. For a while they did not go in but sat in the car watching daylight fade from the long lake view. Suki sat neither near nor far from Henry. His hand over the back of the seat was close to her shoulder, but they did not touch.

"This was a day," he said at last.

"Yes."

"I wonder if this day isn't what it's all about. A day for its own sake. I wonder if this isn't what one spends a lifetime looking for."

"Perhaps. But we didn't find it by looking. It came to us."

Suddenly she moved to him, kissed him at the temple, then jumped out of the car and hurried into the motel.

The next morning she had her bag ready to go by the time he appeared for breakfast. She slept a great deal during the trip to

Boston. When she woke they would exchange a few words before she drifted away again.

"Your brother . . ." she said at one point. "You don't go to see him?"

Henry thought about Joey scrimping through life. "We're very different people."

"Are you angry at one another?"

"No. We're just strangers together."

As they were passing through the traffic around Portsmouth he caught her looking at him. "Do you know how old I am?" he said.

"More or less."

"How old do you think?"

"Not how many years—how old your heart is."

She turned her head away then and perhaps did sleep over the roar of the Interstate beneath the wheels. When they were ten miles from Logan Airport she sat up to watch the congestion of tenant housing and oil depots.

"I also have a mother I didn't go see," he told her.

"In New Hampshire?"

"In Boston."

She said nothing, looking across toward Boston Harbor beyond the airport.

"You didn't ask why."

"It's not for me to ask."

On the plane they were unable to get seats together. When he drove her to her house she shook hands solemnly as she left the car.

After Margo married Henry she went on working conferences and weddings at Airlie House because she liked the people. If it had only been for the money she would have done something else. But the past week's work had brought both fun and good tips. When Henry got home she was running over with good humor. On a Sunday night Sandra and Libby were simultaneously concentrating on TV and homework. Thomas came in briefly for a snack, then disappeared with two other boys. Sounds of a trail bike snarled up from the pasture.

Not until they'd gone to their bedroom did Margo ask about his trip. "How was New Hampshire?"

Henry lay down beside her, not touching her. "I wish you'd come with me." Then he took her in his arms. At first she was rigid, but in time she relaxed a little. He stroked her back, then her hair. He unbuttoned one button and kissed her throat.

"You stay right there," he whispered. He rose, went to the door and listened. The TV was still on. He bellowed to the kids not to stay up too late on a school night. Then he closed the door.

# 7

It began long before Henry recognized it. He'd been running over a gently rolling country road, increasing his distance each morning out by a few yards, on his way from one mile to two. By the first week in August he could do one and five-eighths so long as he did it early, before the sun and the humidity pressed him down into the asphalt.

On August 23, Thomas' fourteenth birthday, he arose with the very first light and went out in running shorts and a T-shirt—plus a baseball cap and a towel to ward off the deerflies.

The air was wet cement. Even the birds were silent. A heavy ground fog lay along the hollows of the pastures. At a mile and a quarter Henry's clothing was soaked, but he was running easily, not suffocated, his feet still light.

There was a slight upgrade at his private marker for a mile and three-eighths (a warping top rail in the four-board fence). He slowed his pace and took it effortlessly, resisting the temptation to sprint a few yards as he topped it. Down the far grade was vanilla, so much like floating that he let himself run past the bridle trail that looped back to the house.

His heart attack had come a dozen years ago, much sooner

than he'd expected it, ten years earlier than his father's first. But he'd burned up his life faster in his martini years. At the time of the event he was forty-five pounds overweight, working up to seventy hours a week (partly to avoid a painful home life), smoking three packs of Larks on short days. He'd been playing tennis with beautiful young men in ninety-degree heat, in a black shirt, bare-headed. When the dizziness came, he'd sat down and lighted a cigarette.

Afterwards, his doctor's instructions were simple: 1) Don't push till it hurts, 2) No more smoking, 3) Don't eat eggs, 4) Exercise moderately and regularly. Rules that had kept him alive for years.

The jog down the grade was spoiled by a deerfly or perhaps two of them circling his head, buzzing in his ear, landing on his neck in hope of rare meat, elevating his ire. Vicious bastards. He draped the towel over his head and shoulders like a kaffiyeh and secured it with his cap. A deerfly landed on the back of his thigh and bit. He killed it with a satisfying smack. While these skirmishes were occurring he passed the one-and-five-eighths point almost without thinking about it. If he turned back now the total distance would be two and a half miles if he cut through the woods. He kept going.

In Suburban Hospital they'd asked about the family history —all bad. Father, three uncles, and a second cousin all dead of coronaries in their fifties. A fourth uncle at forty-eight. Henry had been forty-two that afternoon at Pook's Hill. "You were lucky," they'd said. "A lot of younger men don't live past the first one. The longer you live, the less likely they are to kill you. You've got a lot of miles on you if you do it right." He'd almost killed himself trying to quit smoking and lose weight. "Why should I keep living without tobacco?" he demanded. Edith, to whom he was married at that time, had no answer, but she switched from Pall Malls to Trues.

The one-and-three-quarters-mile mark came at the top of another small rise—a gentle swelling in the earth that reminded Henry of a woman's hip. He circled and started back. As soon as the downgrade ended he reached his limit. It was as though a huge invisible hand were blocking his path. There was no way to run against it. He slowed to a walk—not even a brisk walk. He couldn't draw a deep breath comfortably. Walking very slowly he made it back to the bridle path and turned in, grateful for the woods' shade. His body was running with sweat.

*Humidity's up,* he thought to himself. Even after sunrise the air was hard to breathe—if you could tell when sunrise had come in the Virginia August murk. He told himself he'd try again tomorrow morning.

The years since the early warning had gradually rebuilt his confidence. Marrying Margo had been an act of faith.

At first he'd bought a bike and ridden it all over Shepherd Park, down into the Rock Creek area, alone, then with two-year-old Libby in the baby seat. But an hour of biking a day was eating up his evenings. He was getting bored with it. "Try jogging," said a friend. "One mile is enough for aerobic maintenance."

Not easy. At the start he couldn't run more than fifty paces. He alternated running with walking, stretching it slowly, still not sure what his heart would take.

But then in a month he was up to the mile, and for a decade thereafter he had a second honeymoon with his body, running his twenty minutes at conference and meeting sites all over the country. One wonderful week he did his miles in Salt Lake City, Jacksonville Beach, Cambridge, and Washington's Shepherd Park district, where he and Edith had lived for three years. Until the heart attack his body had seemed useful only for transporting his brain and sexual apparatus. But with renewed confidence brought about by the successful jogging, he and Edith bought the old run-down farm in Sumerduck, where he began chopping and cutting wood, inventing his own carpentry techniques— things he hadn't done since he was a Boy Scout. His weight stayed near 185, his paunch vanished. Yet Pook's Hill was always there in his memory along with his new vocabulary term— myocardial infarction.

One of the things that irritated Henry most about his mind was its lifelong absorption with his own death. He could still remember his childhood terror when first he realized that his breathing could stop forever. How could he risk falling asleep again? He'd lain sweating, fighting off the microdeath that finally forced his eyelids down and bolted them for the night.

"I have a rendezvous with Death" was rhymed almost beyond bearing with "quench my breath." He'd had to memorize it for the Memorial Day exercises at Mason School, attended by his peers and two doddering veterans of the Civil War. The fifth grade sang "Tenting Tonight."

He'd often pictured with delight the scene where Huck Finn and Tom Sawyer were able to sneak into the church balcony to attend their own funeral—the emotional equivalent of drowning in lemon meringue pie. Through too many years of his young manhood he would fall into periodic fantasies about his own funeral—who would come, what would be said—like that early epitaph in the high school yearbook he'd worked so hard to earn:

> *Nickname, Hank* (nobody called him Hank); *Or-chestra,* 2,3,4 (he'd played bass drum and cymbals); *Chronicle,* 3,4 (selling ads); *Student Council,* 4 (no one else in his home room wanted it). . . .

For years after high school he could not shake the mind-set that looked toward a successful obituary, knowing its absurdity, sneering at his own vanity, never quite obliterating it except in rare moments of sexual fulfillment and visits to the coast of Maine.

This peculiar approach to life was eventually complemented by such death-defying acts as smoking and drinking to excess, running short on sleep, participating in dangerous sexual marathons with one of his several wives or others during the interregnums.

But when you marry a woman whose husband has been smashed on a mountain face, there's no more time for self-indulgence in funerary fun and games. In any case a marriage to her and her three children kept him too busy trying to catch his breath to be thinking about dying.

On that August morning of his fifty-fourth year Henry made it home without damaging anything. He even ran the last hundred yards to prove to himself that it had been a non-event. If it was anything, he told himself, it was the humidity or his nerves. He did twenty push-ups on the kitchen floor with no more than the usual puffing.

He still refused to recognize the pattern ten or twenty other times when at a point just under two miles the invisible hand grasped him again. The thing to do obviously was to quit before it happened. No big deal. A year passed during which he ran a mile and a half in comfort. Once, the following spring, he conquered two miles on a cool morning. Progress, he'd thought, but he could never do it again. *Rule 1, don't push till it hurts.*

Each year he'd gone to be shackled with electrodes and march the treadmill (after signing the waiver absolving the doctor and his minions should he collapse on the machine). Each year he demonstrated acceptable stamina and soundness except for the small hitch on the printout that showed the scar tissue from the heart attack at forty-two.

"You've got the right attitude," Dr. Bassett told him. "Live a healthy, energetic life like anyone else. What amazes me, year in and year out, is not how frail the human body is, but how robust. It takes a lot to kill a man." Each year he said the same thing, down to the phrase "year in and year out."

"How does my chart look?" Henry asked the year after he'd run two miles. "Was there something different?"

"The EKG doesn't mean anything without an evaluation of the patient. Are you feeling okay? Are you having any fun? It's important."

"Here's a partial inventory. In the past five years I've married a woman with three teenagers who have demolished two automobiles, a third of my record collection, and the microwave. I have attended forty-four high school football games, become friends with a lot of parents fifteen years younger than I, along with an assortment of traffic cops and judges. I have changed from an insecure, scary job mediating community disputes to a secure, somewhat soporific one as a bureaucrat in the service of my country. I have tripled my sexual activity and joined a quaint religious sect—"

"Which one?"

"The Episcopalians. I have learned to ride a horse, fallen at half the fences in Fauquier County, baled my own hay with a boisterous crew of adolescents, ridden at the tail of a fox hunt, eaten the food of millionaires. . . ."

The doctor looked at him owlishly. "Like I said, are you having any fun?"

"Give me time," said Henry. "I'm thinking."

He thought about it for a week, while he commuted back

and forth on I-66, while jogging, while consuming English muffins and bitter-orange marmalade.

"You don't even know you're eating. What's worrying you?" Margo said on the third morning of this.

"I'm trying to decide whether I'm having any fun. Doctor's orders."

"Tomorrow night at the hunt ball, you'll put on your tux. I'll dress up in a gorgeous gown. We'll eat good food, listen to a great band. You'll dance with beautiful women and get envied by their stuffy husbands for your charm and good looks. Isn't that fun a little bit?"

Henry looked dubious.

"You Yankees!" Margo exploded. "You analyze everything to death. It's a wonder you can even make love."

"I've been thinking about that, too."

"Stop! Right this instant! I bet you've even planned your own funeral."

"Many times."

"You're having more than one?"

"I keep revising."

"That must be fun."

Margo couldn't even plan a shopping trip, but she knew fun when it came along. That spring she went with Henry to find a new used car to replace the old dying used car. Henry had never bought a new car, getting even with Detroit in his own way.

"Craig loved his Monte Carlo," she said. "It was sharp, but it could take us all to church without making us blush."

They test-drove a Monte Carlo. It pitched like a galleon.

"Bad shocks," Henry said as they took it back.

In one corner of the lot a Triumph TR6 was sunning itself. Its paint was chocolate with silver racing stripes. It had new

Michelin red-wall tires on its wheels and nineteen thousand miles on its odometer.

"It has neck-snapping torque," the salesman said.

"It looks like a Hershey bar," Margo said. "Why don't you try it?"

The keys materialized in Henry's hand, and they were floating out Route 211 toward the Blue Ridge Mountains. The TR6 smiled like a cat getting its back scratched whenever Henry touched the gas pedal. Black dials with green numerals were set in a lustrous hardwood dashboard. Its exhaust spat insults at other cars.

Lost in testing, shifting, feeling, Henry suddenly realized Margo was grinning at him.

"What?" he said crossly.

"You know what."

"The kids would wreck it in a week."

"Don't let them use it."

"You mean, not share it?"

"Yes, Henry! You're entitled to keep something to yourself. It's your house. You pay the bills."

"It only holds two people."

"Marty has his own car. The others can ride with him or their friends. Or they can use the truck."

"It would probably hold its value."

"It doesn't have to. It's a toy."

"But forty-eight hundred bucks—"

"We can afford it. We'll take it out of the bank. We'll hand them cash."

"If we ever needed the money I could sell it."

"You won't even sell the junk behind the barn."

It was true. There was no point in buying more white elephants. Henry turned the TR6 around, took it back to its orphanage, handed the keys to the salesman, looked bleakly toward a row of practical Toyotas and Volkswagens.

"We'll take it," Margo said.

Henry bought a hat with a long bill and drove the TR6 back and forth to work in Washington, wrestling the top up and down as required by the showers of April, complaining the whole time.

"You're having fun," Margo told him. "Try to keep that in mind."

One evening coming home in June a punk kid in a battered pickup truck played tag with the TR6, much to Henry's annoyance. It had been a bad day. Fifty thousand copies of his agency's urgent publications had been discovered sitting on a loading dock for two weeks. The air was close, the fumes heavy, the sun merciless even at seven. Henry wished he'd left the top up. He wished the kid would stop cutting in front of him. The kid had spiky hair dyed orange and a smudged upper lip. A stalled truck on I-66 brought traffic to a standstill with the TR6 and the pickup truck side by side. The kid's head was eighteen inches above Henry's head. They exchanged a long silent look up and down.

"Great wheels," the kid said abruptly.

"Thank you."

"Someday I'm gonna get me a set of wheels like that."

"Yeah," Henry said. "Do it. Fun car." He restrained himself from racing the engine.

He'd been stuck at one mile all summer, but he could do it without discomfort if he got out before the sun burned through the morning haze. September passed and the skies cleared. The mornings were new apples. Henry tried for a mile and a quarter. No good.

The invisible hand was waiting at the one-mile mark. It was simply impossible to run beyond it. Nothing hurt, exactly. Rather, his lungs refused to accept any more air. He slowed to a walk.

Next morning he jogged a little slower, determined to break a mile if only by ten yards. The hand stopped him fifty yards short of the mile mark. Angry, breathless, he walked a slow hundred yards, then ran the final fifty. When he finished it his lungs didn't want to breathe at all. There was a dull pain in his diaphragm — from the struggle to force the air in, he told himself.

You're internalizing your emotions again, he told himself. It was a chaotic adolescent time at home, a sludgelike time of bureaucratic treacle at the office. None of it bounced off Henry's hide. It entered through all his mucous membranes and lodged in his alimentary canal. Nothing passed comfortably through its locks.

By October he had compromised and settled for three quarters of a mile. Anything more brought back the sensations in his diaphragm.

One morning in early November Margo went out to run with him. At half a mile he stopped to walk.

"What's wrong?" she said.

"A little slow this morning."

"A little? I thought you were running two miles."

"Last year."

Three mornings later he was on Dr. Bassett's treadmill with Margo in the waiting room. After six minutes Henry stopped the test, feeling faint.

"What hurts?" the doctor said.

"Nothing really. Just sort of pooped and dizzy."

"Where does it hurt?"

"Well . . . it doesn't hurt, exactly. Just this heaviness in my diaphragm."

"How long have you been getting that?"

Henry shrugged. "A year maybe? A little more . . ."

"Dummy!" Dr. Bassett shouted. "Don't you know what that is? Angina, that's what."

Henry had heard of it but didn't realize it was pronounced to rhyme with vagina. "So?" he said.

"So you stop running, you dope. I'll give you some pills. Walk, don't run. Come back in two weeks."

Henry and Margo took the day off. They drove the TR6 into Washington and parked it on the Mall. Yellow leaves were strewn on the grass, glowing in the clear sunlight.

"Where do we start?" Henry said.

"I've got to get to the john." Margo headed toward the National Gallery with Henry in tow.

When they met in the foyer Henry could hardly contain his excitement. "I have just seen the most magnificent urinals in Washington," he told her. "Truly, these are works of art— capacious, stately, they should be in a Greek temple."

Margo gave him a slantwise look. "Want to find coffee somewhere?"

"Dear woman, you aren't taking me seriously. These urinals must have come from a Mellon mansion somewhere. They've given me a magnificent idea. I'll be the talk of the art world."

He was standing in the center of the foyer, waving his arms. Fortunately there were no other visitors at this moment. She led the way outside, looked across Constitution Avenue past the bow of the Federal Trade Commission building in search of a restaurant, eventually settled them in a Jewish delicatessen called the Blarney Stone on Pennsylvania Avenue—noisy, bright, flyspecked, the sort of place where you worried about the coleslaw.

"There's one I should get over on Eastern Neck," Henry said as the waitress took Margo's order.

"One what?"

"A urinal. I think it must have been made in Europe. It has a flush tank set on the back of it, and the receptacle is the shape of a nebbish face, but it's about the height of a conventional toilet. This is not a joke, Margo. I could become the world's leading expert on urinal art. It's an untouched field. Picture me on the *Today* show—"

"Henry."

His attention wavered, stopped, came back to her.

"What did the doctor say?"

He shrugged. "Angina. He gave me a prescription. People live with it for years."

"But what does it mean? What did he say about your heart? Isn't angina supposed to hurt a lot? Are you supposed to stop running or what? You just can't ignore it, Henry."

But he wasn't hearing her, slouched back in the corner of the booth. "Tell me," he said. "Do you realize the incredible diversity? I've seen them made of porcelain, soapstone, aluminum, corrugated galvanized iron, plastic. Just within the federal buildings there are endless variations. I think I'll need a wide-angle lens. What if I do some with the user community in attendance. God, think of the mob scene at the Kennedy Center!"

The prescription was Isordil. It made Henry sick. It gave him headaches, upset his digestion, depressed him severely. It exhausted him. At the end of a day it was almost more than he could manage to drive the forty miles home. Several nights he had to pull off to rest. When he did get home he went to bed immediately after supper, slept sluggishly, dreamed nightmares, woke with a head full of wool.

After a week he threw the pills away. "Goddam doctors. They're worse than the disease. I was fine until I went to the goddam doctor."

Nor would he quit the jogging. If half a mile was the limit, then he'd run the half and walk the rest. The end of autumn was his favorite time of year. By late November the leaves had lost the last of their brilliance. Thick quilts of them lay fragrantly in hollows of fields or along the woods' edge where northwest winds had driven them, save for those queer brown breechclouts of quivering oak clusters that would cling to the waists of their trees until new life would break them loose in March.

Henry carefully steered a mental course away from where he might be by March. November mornings had a spice that cleared the brain and eyes. Cold enough for a sweat suit, clear enough that deciduous twigs stood out from their branches like wire, crazing the borders of the lemon morning sky. Each new day was the strike of a chime for Henry, filling him with unreasoning happiness in his body's walking and running the earth's crust as his endurance permitted.

Evenings were less good as his heart's insufficiency decreased the oxygen supply to muscles and vital organs. He came to dread the forty-mile commute home to Broad Run at the end of a day in the bureaucratic squirrel wheel that was his job. Some evenings it was all he could do to finish dinner before he fell into bed.

Dr. Bassett had him try transdermal applications of Isordil, but an hour after the paste was applied to his belly all the flu symptoms reappeared.

"You're not in any immediate danger," the doctor told him. "Keep these nitroglycerine tablets with you. Slip one in by your gum if you get any angina problems."

For as long as he could, Henry avoided telling Margo about

symptoms, the latest diagnosis, the outlook for the months ahead. When he could, he avoided thinking about it himself.

Finally she forced the issue. "I can deal with trouble," she told him. "I just have to know what it is. Remember, I've lost one husband when my back was turned—"

"What do you want to know?" he said uncomfortably.

"How bad it is. What can be done. How risky it is. I've been reading about open-heart surgery—do you want to see my scrapbook?"

"No thank you. Every time I go see Bassett he draws me a diagram of my heart and gives me the same anatomy lesson."

"So what does he tell you?"

"He wants me to get through Christmas and New Year's. Then I'll go in for an angiogram."

"That's not dangerous—waiting?"

"I asked him that. He says it's dangerous crossing Pennsylvania Avenue. He's said that to me at least five times. I get the feeling he has trouble telling one patient from another without their charts."

"Makes you feel special, doesn't it?"

"I remember once I went in for an upper GI series. I was known as the stomach in 3B."

Margo went to hug him. "I'll come and stay with you—if I can remember your name."


Henry put off the angiogram until almost June, rationalizing all the while. He told himself that as long as he could run half a mile there must be at least marginal coronary circulation. When the weather made running outdoors impossible he jogged around the house in his stocking feet.

In March Margo discovered the Pritikin book and put Henry on a rigid regime of vegetables and rice, damn little meat, and no fat at all—or as close as he could come to it. It was rudimentary eating, but it seemed to raise Henry's strength for a while. As April woke the earth he found he could run almost a mile if he jogged easily and stayed relaxed. He almost believed in Pritikin's remission claims. His arteries and veins felt cool and clear when his body passed through the gentle movement of the morning air.

This was the most precious April of his life. The small parcels of woods scattered along the roadway with fields flowing among them seemed like the islands of Lake Winnipesaukee. Henry had lost all sense of time as the lake's lover years ago, loving her best on April's solitary mornings when the last ice crystals were newly gone and he could look deeply into her waters to the shadowed, calm world of bass and perch and dark glacial boulders. Now the ground of these Virginia mornings was like a lake beneath his feet. He felt that if he looked down he would be able to see into that earth's skeleton as though it were water glowing beneath a boat hull.

In the new sunlight of an April morning even the gravel road had beauty, each crushed rock fragment throwing a shadow seven times its height, mountain ranges to the early worm.

Henry inhaled happily—the cool air, pure as spring water to his nostrils, rushed deep into his lungs.

In Virginia the seasons correspond to the calendar. This is not true in New England where New Hampshire's high hillside woods can harbor granular snowpacks into May or in Vermont where mud time sometimes seems determined to swallow spring entirely.

But in Virginia it is done correctly. Autumns linger almost into Christmas with here and there an unexpected Indian summer afternoon in December.

And spring comes when it should, often warming early in March. Snow still may come—enormous, viscous, sodden storms that seem to fall in clumps to cling to shovels or choke a plow like bread dough. In a day or two it sluices away in rainstorms or is melted like detergent suds by strident sunshine that bustles in for a steaming day that amazes no one but the keepers of the weather records on the evening news.

But this was April almost into May, and Henry's solitary mornings popped with birdsong, sounds almost visible—not only the sparrows and woodpeckers and cardinals that had swung the feeder through the winter months, but a killdeer now, and warblers like decks of spattering cards. Soon barn swallows and red-winged blackbirds. Already Henry had caught his annual fleeting glimpse of a Baltimore oriole high in a group of hickory trees still budding their first foliage. Its luscious song was like a teasing lover—find me if you can. Two years ago he had seen a scarlet tanager about this week in April—his only look in a lifetime.

These were hours to love the earth alone, away from a wife's protective love or from adolescent alarums. Henry even left the dog behind in his greed for solitude.

Not that the family was not a warm home base. The kids' concern—perhaps with prodding by Margo in the wings—took the form of touching, uncharacteristic offers of timely assistance. *Let me get the wood in, Dad. . . . Here, put that shovel down.*

Henry, of course, hung on to more than he could manage until fatigue sneaked up and buffeted him. Just once when a chest cramp caught him unaware he let his guard down enough to drop a nitroglycerine tablet by his gum. In four minutes the tablet was gone—and Henry had a hatchet blade of pain buried in the front of his skull.

May and warmer days shortened his tether. Only on very

good mornings could he jog for even half a mile. In Salt Lake City he ventured forth from the Little America Hotel, where he was chairing a meeting, to find he couldn't run four blocks. He couldn't even keep to a walk but leaned against a power pole until his head stopped swimming.

"They'll keep you overnight to be sure the artery is sealed," Dr. Bassett had told him.

Henry sat on the edge of the hospital bed, still fully dressed, waiting for instructions. Eight-twenty. He'd left home at six to beat the traffic across the Roosevelt Bridge.

"Washington Hospital Center looks like an Army post in the desert, but don't let that fool you," the doctor had said. "They've got a team of heart surgeons who could replumb a mouse. Don't take my word for it; go there for your angiogram and judge for yourself."

Henry waited, reading through the admissions pack. First item was a Patient's Bill of Rights. Good human relations. He kicked off his shoes, raised the head of his bed to a comfortable slope, lay back, and dozed, remembering as he drifted off a similar protective drowsiness under shellfire in a hillside dugout thirty-five years before.

The cardiologist woke him and listened to his heart. He was a gaunt, sepulchral German with a graveside humor that Henry found irresistible. "Vell," he said. "Still limping along? Ve'll vake it up with a special cocktail. You want the lecture? Diagram? No? Vas you here last veek?"

Henry grinned at him. "I've never seen you in my life before."

The doctor shook hands somberly. "Ernst Heinzelmann.

That translates, if you should vonder, to one of those little men who comes in the night and spins your flax into gold. Appropriate, no?"

"Gnome," said Henry. "But you're too lanky."

"Oh, vell. In der operating room I vear my viskers. . . . You do understand vat happens, don't you? Ve make you relaxed but not asleep. Ve hook you up to nine hundert sensors, and I have five members of the Vashington Redskins who vatch the dials. Ve run a probe through your femoral artery—you know vere? Good—up through into the aorta and to your heart. There ve release a dye which vill make you feel hot all over, and the heat'll go directly to your anus. I do not know vy, so don't ask me that.

"The dye enables us to see and take pictures of your coronary arteries. Ve can measure and precisely locate any blockage you may have. Then ve ship you back here, park a truck on your thigh to seal the artery, and tell you not to move the leg for nineteen days."

"How long, really?"

"Oh, six hours, maybe. Ve don't want you messing up the sheets with your blood, there."

Then came a pretty nurse to tell Henry that Dr. Heinzelmann was a genius in goat's clothing. Henry's loins were shaved. He was sedated and floated up to a sanctuary crowded with X-ray machines, pumps, pipes, gleaming dials and monitor screens, and, indeed, four burly men in green gowns, masks, and sneakers. Their eyes glowed in the dark like wolves'. Henry liked the sneakers.

Then finally Dr. Ernst Heinzelmann in gown and mask but no sneakers, talking and talking softly and quietly, a reassuring hand on Henry's arm, pointing out the monitor where Henry could see, by rolling his eyes up, the wavering probe, like a cat's whisker in the picture, winding through his arteries toward his heart.

Then the dye. The doctor announced it and it felt exactly as he'd said it would.

"So fast!" Henry said. "Like setting fire to gasoline vapor." He was drenched in sweat under the gown. Then cold suddenly.

The doctor gripped his arm. "Cough!"

Henry coughed.

"Again! Cough hard!" The hand shook his arm.

Henry coughed as well as he could, but his breath was sloppy and bees were buzzing in his ears. "I may pass out," he tried to say, but the words stuck on his tongue.

The hand relaxed. "Okay now. Take a good breath. Your head will clear."

The night was a sarcophagus, lying rigid under dire strictures not to move, but he couldn't have moved if he tried. Finally after much itching he slept.

"Vell, ve let you go pretty soon. Vere's your vife?" Morning sun flooded the room.

"Home. I just talked to her."

"You driving home alone? How far? Two t'ousand miles? You must be one of those big daddy type A's. No vunder you got chest pains."

Henry stared at the owlish face.

"It's probably okay. Just take it easy as you go—but first ve talk. This time you get to see the diagram again vedder you like it or not." He spread a map of Henry's heart out on the sheet. "Here's vy you get angina. You have two coronary arteries blocked seventy percent. Here and here. One eighty percent here. One ninety percent here. Maybe a fifth. Ve're not sure. Ve t'ink you ought to do something about it. One of those babies closes up, you go out pretty fast."

Henry took a deep breath. "How soon?"

"As soon as you can make yourself accept it and ve can schedule you. The boys are doing them like sardines now. Piece of cake."

"What's the risk?"

"Here—in this pile of bricks—less than one percent. Check it out. Ask everyone who can give you intelligent advice. If you don't like us, go some odder place. But don't put it off too long. Vit the angiogram you've already been through the scariest part. In surgery you have a long sleep. A whole veek to vake up decently."

"I meant to ask you—what was all that cough business?"

"Oh, that. Your heart stopped ven the dye hit it. The coughing makes a pumping action till the heart vakes up."

"My heart actually stopped?"

"Sure. That's why you started to pass out. No sweat. I could have cranked it up with digitalis. Just easier by coughing."

There was a man—the deputy secretary—who'd had bypass surgery. Henry sent a request through channels to spend an hour with him, specifying the subject matter. In a day the response came back. "Be in his office by seven tomorrow morning."

Henry took a hotel room to be there on time. This was a rare man: a tailor's son from Brooklyn who'd graduated with honors from Yale, switched from music to sociology and got a Ph.D. from Columbia. He'd been president of two universities and now headed Henry's department and all seventy thousand of its employees.

His office was enormous. Henry took in a landscape of walnut paneling, leather couches and chairs, an oil by Inness, braided flags, glassed-in bookcases. Eating grapefruit at his desk was Deputy Secretary Sam Warshaw, wearing Adidas running shoes, slacks, a dress shirt open two buttons at the neck, no undershirt. A man conscious of his appearance — gray beard, a good head of gray hair blown-dry, black eyebrows, airline pilot's glasses. A man who would love to talk. His whole body resonated to Henry's presence.

He rose, came to Henry, shook hands. "Excuse me. I didn't expect you so soon." He led Henry to a coffee table surrounded by a couch and easy chairs. "Decaffeinated, I presume? Please excuse my footgear. I run before it gets hot."

"I do, too." Henry was aware of witnessing a performance and liked it in spite of himself.

"So you're facing a bypass? Have you decided on it? How can I help you?" The voice was musical, just short of theatrical.

Henry listened to his own breathing for a minute. Tasted the coffee: good enough not to need cream.

"I called the surgical team at Washington Hospital Center yesterday afternoon. I made an appointment for June 10. Then I went to Raleigh's and ordered a three-piece suit that will be ready for delivery the eighteenth."

"Wonderful! Then you need me just as a tour guide." He threw his hands in the air, beaming at Henry. A young man in a white serving jacket came on silent feet, bringing fresh coffee and orange juice.

"I'll share my experience with you because it will ease your mind this morning. But if I didn't tell you anything, you'd get through it perfectly well. It is not a piece of cake as the doctors universally tell you, but it is manageable. You can deal with the pain, and it's not so bad with all the drugs you'll get. But let me interrupt myself to say simply that you were invited here because your colleagues believe you are a valuable person not only professionally but as a human being." He paused and looked Henry directly in the eye—popped his own eyes. "Savor that, my friend. We don't get love letters like that often enough."

Here at last was an epitaph he'd daydreamed for himself, but when it came Henry couldn't deal with it. As he had always done, he cringed at the compliment, feeling simultaneously flattered and annoyed. "I'm at a loss for words," he said, trying not to look sour.

"Don't analyze it." The deputy secretary got to his feet to pace, coffee cup in hand. "I'm sure you've been briefed on the process. They lower your temperature. They open you up like a rack of lamb. They take vein tissue from your leg and manufacture for you a new coronary artery system. Mine was five —out of a possible seven—four years ago. The chest scar starts at the top of the sternum here and goes to within three inches of the navel. The scar on my right leg—actually three long scars—starts midcalf and comes fully to the groin. I hated the scars at first. I wouldn't swim. But I've come to a point of affection for them. They've faded now. They'll never be beautiful but they're my battle ribbons."

"It's funny," Henry said. "I didn't think I'd be concerned about my physical appearance in my mid-fifties, but that seems to be one of the things that worries me most."

"Oh, yes indeed—and why not? Are we supposed to become prunes at fifty? I'm very much a sensual animal. I hope I never stop."

"How long does it take—getting well—after being opened up like that?"

"This is a miracle procedure, my friend. They told me the color in my coronary tissues—and in my face—improved dramatically while my chest was still open. I was on my feet twenty-four hours after I got out of intensive care. I was walking a cumulative twenty minutes a day a week later when I left the hospital. I was back to work five weeks after surgery.

"I have a mild chronic edema of the right ankle. . . . For the first few months I could feel the two halves of my breastbone shifting. The danger is more perceived than actual. Your heart muscle will be past most of the danger in three weeks. Your sternum in eight. Your greatest challenge will be to believe in your heart again." His hands were continually in motion as he spoke. He underscored words with his head, his body. He watched Henry closely for reactions. "The hardest time will be right at the beginning in intensive care, but this will be much harder for your wife than for you because you'll be so heavily sedated. You'll have a nurse at your side constantly at the beginning. Her face will fill your consciousness. She will be beautiful. You will fall in love with her. . . . At the outset you will have an endotracheal tube that feels like an Electrolux hose down your throat. It is unpleasant. It stays about eighteen hours. It makes communication almost impossible. You may want to work out a simple eye-blink code in advance with your wife to tell her if something hurts so she can play twenty questions with you. In my case it was my heels—you're flat on your back for the first several days. After some struggle I got a pillow placed under my calves. I still can feel that ache in my heels, remembering it."

He came back to sit on his couch, absently reaching inside his shirt and massaging the muscles of his shoulder.

"Your wife will be briefed on what to expect: the long wait—

up to eight hours—though she'll get bulletins. In the intensive care unit she'll see you with tubes growing out of you everywhere, monitors all around. She will become terrified when she sees your heart's telemetry showing irregularity as it may for the first day or two. She will hear you yelp when they remove the abdominal drains—they make scars, too. . . ." He lapsed into silence, sorting through the images in his head. His eyes traveled back and forth, watching them. He sat back deep into the couch for a minute, arms behind his head. Then he jumped up again to pace, to peer out through the curtained windows to the street.

"This is my fourth tour in Washington. My third in this department. There are a great many people I love here, people I've known in some cases for more than twenty years. This hit me suddenly last week at the retirement party of one of the division chiefs in the Office of Higher Education where I spent so much time.

"As the jokes and tributes came and went, I stood at the back of the room and watched the faces and bodies of these familiar people—many I'd first known as junior aides, hardly out of college, now balding and graying, carrying great responsibility, driven by it, and by the terrible frustration of the bureaucratic dragon in whose bowels we toil. Dead people unaware that they'd gone and left their bodies to live out their juiceless lives."

He circled around to where Henry was sitting, delighted with the picture he'd painted. *This is a performance,* Henry thought. In spite of himself he was irritated by the display of vanity. He'd hoped for a bit of quiet dialog, not a peroration. For a minute he thought the deputy secretary was going to lean down and take him by the shoulders, but he resumed pacing.

"I remembered again my promise to myself when I was reborn on that operating table—to realize my life for all the days that I should still have it—to stop the discounting, the procrastination, the false and grudging generosity, the false humility—and to do what it took to make myself a living person, whatever the cost, whatever the risk. In my case it was music. I am composing a symphony—and fishing in Canada, in the face of other obligations to my job and to my family."

He stopped and peered at Henry who was staring glumly off into the distance. "Where did I lose you?" Henry's common courtesy made him conceal his annoyance. If the great man was putting on a show it was, after all, for Henry's benefit. The least he could do was try to be grateful. "You didn't lose me. I lost myself."

"Oh? How's that?"

"You know what?" Henry said. "All through these past months I've just shut the reality out—first the fact that anything was wrong, then the tests, the diagnoses, the prospect of whatever I'm going to be when it's all over. Instead I made up this whole game about urinals—I was going to do a photo essay on urinals. I was going to become the leading consultant in the world on urinal art. My wife doesn't see the humor in it."

The deputy secretary nodded, dead-pan. "It would be less funny to a woman."

"I didn't even want to see you. As soon as I asked, I wished I hadn't. I resented you for inviting me here. As you've been talking I've resented you for being so goddam vigorous, if you'll forgive my saying so. The only reason I made the decision to have the surgery was because I couldn't stand the thought of being a cardiac cripple."

"You think you're the only one who felt all that crap?" The deputy secretary came and stood over Henry. "Until this minute you've been living your entire life to die, because your father had a bad heart and died too soon. Tell me I'm wrong."

They stared at each other. Henry was silent.

"Now you can change that. You are literally about to be reborn. Now you can live for living, dream new dreams, harvest the fruit you never imagined could be within your reach. Stop living for others. It never works anyhow. Live to please yourself. There's only one catch."

Henry looked at him over his glasses, waiting.

"Someday you give what I've just given you to someone else."

The evening of June 7 was clear and warm. A single bag was packed for Henry's trip. He was due at the hospital the next afternoon.

He pulled down the top of the TR6 and snapped the boot neatly into place, told Margo he'd be back in an hour and drove out into the erotic evening Virginia had prepared for him. In the distance the Blue Ridge skyline rose and fell as the little car swept up and down the grades. The dance reminded Henry of barn swallows looping around his tractor when he mowed, stirring up thousands of bugs for them to catch.

He turned right at 688, drove up through Orlean, left to Hume—minute hamlets—left again up winding narrow roads toward Flint Hill. These were the roadways a British sports car is made for. Henry's jaws could feel its bite on the turns.

The air had been glorious for a week. He saw windrows of raked hay—or bales waiting for pickup, tossed about like gold-wrapped candy bars against the new-mown grass. The perfume of the pastures filled his head. As dusk descended, the evening hands of women touched his cheek and played with his collar and about his neck and shoulders.

. . .

It was after ten when he coasted into the driveway at home, threw the tonneau cover over the car, bounced into the house, went directly to the bookcase in his den.

Margo heard the door. "Honey?" she called. "Is that you?"

Henry emerged, volume in hand. "Do you realize," he said in outrage, "that the goddam *Encyclopedia Britannica* doesn't even have an entry under *urinal?*"

# 8

---

Margo stayed four nights in the nurses' quarters until Henry was out of intensive care. It was absurd to think her presence had anything to do with keeping him alive, but she couldn't permit herself to feel secure. The memory of the night Craig was killed was rekindled. She saw herself again, as she placed the phone in its cradle and sat on the edge of her bed with her arms crossed over her breasts, holding herself together.

The first thing she'd thought about was that she hadn't picked up Craig's shirts. Then she couldn't concentrate on anything for a while. She felt laced too tight to breathe. She went down to the kitchen and sat on one of the stools by the breakfast bar, waiting. Perhaps if she waited they'd call back and tell her it was a mistake, someone else with a similar name. All the lights were burning but she had no memory of turning them on. When the phone rang she'd been asleep in her bed—perhaps fitfully because he was overdue and the wind was high. She hated April.

Although she knew it was not a mistake her mind kept wanting to deny it, like a bird repeatedly trying to fly through a pane of plate glass.

There were no clouds but the wind had howled for two days.

Twice it had blown the pasture gate completely off its hinges. Margo and both boys together had fought it back into place. The second time they lashed it with lead shanks and a lunge line. They'd had to fight the horses into the barn first. The horses didn't like the wind, either, not blowing and blowing that way. It was unnatural.

She thought that if the wind dropped she would be able to cry. It was like food poisoning of the spirit. Like being sick to death and needing to vomit and not being able to straighten up. She sat on the stool by the breakfast bar and looked at the telephone on the wall just above her head.

The April wind blew across the top of the fieldstone chimney, making it howl like a bottle. It blew the smell of dead fire and creosote back into the room. The house was a large A-frame with fourteen-foot ceilings and slanted walls and a wall of windows looking east down beyond the pasture and barn to fields that would be tall with corn in August. The boys and Sandra had rooms in the basement area, so they had not heard the phone.

She had hated his flying. She had hated flying with him, with all five of them, Thomas airsick in the back and Marty navigating them in and out of disaster, with Craig alternately yelling and laughing at him.

Risk was a way of life for all of them. Sandra was fox hunting when she was seven, when she was so small that all you could see was the pony's ears approaching the far side of a big coop. Once Margo had slid thirty feet under Brandy when Brandy's front hoof went into a groundhog hole. When anybody rode off you never said, "Be careful." You said, "Have fun."

When Craig went off for a trip in the Cessna she didn't say, "Have fun." She watched as he drove out the front gate.

She knew she would have to call someone but she could not make her arm raise her hand to the telephone. The house was cold with the wind blowing and made her shiver. Not the bad shaking—that would begin later, toward dawn, lying alone in her sweatsuit under the electric blanket, shaking as though she were only bones and the wind could blow through her. Off and on she would have fits of shaking for weeks.

She couldn't remember putting her sweat suit on, either. Maybe she'd gone to bed in it.

The phone had rung just after one. When she'd answered it the man gave his name and said he was the coroner of Mitchell County, North Carolina. There had been an accident. He had asked if she was Mrs. Craig Bishop first.

"Are you sure there's no mistake?" she kept saying.

"No, ma'am. We have all his papers. Craig Martin Bishop, Jr."

But she wouldn't accept it. "Could you describe him?"

"I'm sorry, ma'am. There was a fire. We do have his rings."

After that she must have come downstairs, turning on all the lights, even the floodlights over the deck and back toward the driveway.

On the breakfast bar were Marty's books sprawled from a pile, the salt and pepper shakers in the form of lighthouses, Thomas' sneakers, and a grape jelly smear where Marty had made his sandwiches. Margo took a paper napkin from the stack and carefully wiped up the spilled jelly. She folded the jelly into the napkin, then folded it again and again until it wouldn't bend any more.

She realized that a song had been going through her head: "Buona Sera," Louis Prima's antic voice echoing in her ears.

She would have to call his mother first. His mother would be hysterical. She remembered sensing a note of relief in the coroner's voice when he realized she wasn't going to be hysterical.

But she couldn't bring herself to say words yet. She couldn't make it real. She couldn't allow herself to think of her children asleep in their rooms.

She slipped down from the stool and walked slowly around the room switching off lights one by one until just the floodlights outside were left, spilling shards of brightness back into the living room. After a moment she turned the floodlights off, too.

Fourth year, fourth month, fourth day. She sat on the stones of the raised hearth with her back to the cold fireplace and waited for her eyes to work. There was more than half a moon. Already she could see the shape of the barn below the house.

The wind rose until she could feel the timbers of the house thrumming under her feet. Only children could sleep through this. Only her children could. Thomas had once slept through a four-car collision.

She slid the glass door open to go out onto the deck but had to retreat. Even at fifty degrees the wind chill ate through her sweat suit.

From a pile on the couch she dug out Marty's down jacket and put it on, stepped onto the deck, then down the stairs. She climbed the fence, fighting the wind for balance, and ran the ninety feet to the cover of the barn. The aisleway ran north and south so that the northwest wind was not blowing directly in, but the whole structure was quaking on its cement foundations. The horses were edgy.

With only the overhead lights from the aisle burning, Margo slipped into Brandy's stall and stroked his neck to comfort him. She could feel his warmth. His smell was warm and leathery like a good purse.

She stood beside him with her arm there and imagined herself tacking him up, riding him out into the moonlight, into the flickering darkness of the woods below Max Engelhardt's farm with the wind tearing at Brandy's mane and her own hair.

Then Craig was in the stall with them. She could feel his presence as though he had put his hand on her shoulder. But she knew that if she turned to look at him he would be gone.

Now Henry. The day of his operation she had stood by his bed, watching his chest rise and fall, watching for the color in his face, until his first stirrings of consciousness, the faint pressure of his hand in hers. He would live. She could believe it now. But still she waited a little before she called the children.

# PART

# II

# 9

Sandra was the only one who had said yes when Henry offered to adopt them. The boys were afraid they'd have to change their name. When it was explained that they had the option they were still uncomfortable. Henry never mentioned it, but Margo knew he hadn't forgotten it ten years later.

Margo still truly felt God had sent Henry to her because he was stable and attractive and funny in his perverse Yankee way — and a good lover, though it was difficult for him to be demonstrative.

He still had trouble hugging people, an act that was the most natural thing in the world for Margo, who hugged everybody. Before they were married, Margo in her effervescence would embrace a man casually at a hunt breakfast or stand talking with her arms around him while Henry steamed in a corner. Once, when one of them patted her bottom, Henry had walked out and stood in the garden by himself.

"They're just old friends," she told him. "It doesn't mean anything. These people saved my life after Craig died."

"You just walk off and leave me," Henry had said. "I don't know a soul and you're letting some guy feel you up."

It had made Margo angry, but she felt so secure about herself in those days that she could dismiss it. Once she had bragged to Henry that she'd been the world's champion mother and married lady, and it wasn't far from the truth. When Marty had been little she'd had the biggest Cub Scout den in Fauquier County and took them on trips and played with them as though they were dolls, almost.

Now there was a different problem. Henry had stopped being jealous. He was always kind, if a bit tart at times. But he'd been more loving in their earlier days—at least more spontaneous. The heart surgery had been startlingly successful. He was more vigorous even than when they'd first met. But now he was always under control. When he was under control it made Margo feel shaky inside. This interplay was the balance wheel and hairspring of their relationship—the escapement through which time and emotional discharge fired from second to second, and would go on so until the power source eventually wore out.

If it was a game, Henry seemed to get better at it. He made fewer errors, was toppled less frequently by opposing players. But Margo was falling behind, becoming less skillful and more vulnerable as one after another of the children branded her ineffectual or unstable—or, worse still, left home while their beds were still warm.

The only thing worse than having Sandra there was having her gone. Nothing left a bigger lump in Margo's throat than to find Sandra's chaotic room as empty as an egg crate. Only her occasional forays home to drive her mother crazy kept Margo sane.

When Sandra had chosen a mate at twenty-one, Margo was convinced at once that the selection was made expressly with the design of pushing her over the brink. Tall, slim, elegant with a pencil-line mustache, Ed Clarendon was one of those Floridians whose conspicuous religion was the worship of their own bodies. Ed drove a Jaguar. When one of the cats walked on it during his first visit, he whipped out a dustcover and patted it into place over his car's voluptuous fenders. After Thomas, Margo didn't think she could take it.

"Her Ed has no sense of humor," she told Henry.

"I haven't met a Jaguar owner who does."

"All he thinks of is his looks. He told me he gets that tan from a sunlamp now that he's left Florida."

"He'll fit into this family perfectly."

"He's a Republican. He works for that conservative congressman from the Tidewater."

Henry sighed. He'd hoped for at least one Democrat.

Ed was great in bed, though, Sandra told them in her candor. Then she committed the unpardonable sin. She conceived on her wedding night, and Margo was a grandmother before the last of the wedding bills were paid.

"I will not be Grandma," she told Henry. All her life she'd had to be what other people told her she was. As a small girl she'd been the White Roach because she was the only fair child in the family. Then Tank as a teenager. And in succession:

Dizzy Legs

Butter-Brain

Old Faithful

Super Mom

as friends and relatives viewed her qualities and tagged her for what they thought they'd seen.

Finally her children pronounced her mad and left her to deal with it. She did the best she could, grabbing wisdom where she found it—in a copy of *Ms.* at the hairdressers, from a Leo Buscaglia book, and finally at a few sessions with a warm-hearted counselor who told her to look inside herself.

She did a series of pencil studies of her own face, ranging in mood from tragic to saucy, switched to acrylics for a still life, tried a charcoal of Henry, settled finally for pastels—a painful self-portrait full of purple shadows and orange and green flesh tones, full of rage, full of defiance.

She howled that she was damned if she would become a little gray lady with her hair in a bun. Yet there was Sandra whelping at every opportunity.

Margo and her three-year-old grandson Eric were taking a bath. Margo soaped the cloth and handed it to him. "Wash," she said.

"Where?"

"Where would you like to start?"

"You do it."

Margo took the washcloth back and started with his chest since it was within reach.

"Ow!" screamed Eric.

Margo stopped and stared at him without rancor. With the heel of his left hand he made a small semicircular motorboat wake.

"Either you've got to wash or let me do it."

Eric stared down into the water, then up into her eyes. He sang:

> More than meets the eyes,
> I don't bot stake paro judys . . .

"What's that?"

"A song," he said with elaborate patience. His hair was as pale as his skin, particularly so when wet. In the tub it was difficult to tell whether his nose was still running.

"Where did you hear it?"

"What?" Being deaf was a game he played and she was getting sick of it. It had gone on all through supper.

"You heard me."

"On TV."

She had meanwhile resoaped the cloth. She seized his head and proceeded vigorously to wash his neck and ears.

"Ow! Ow, Grandmommy Margo! Ow!"

She leaned back to observe the effect. Although she was still a long way from being ready to accept grandparenthood, she did know exactly how to push a child through its ablutions.

"What's that?" he said pointing.

"My fuzzies."

Eric giggled. "Mommy has fuzzies, too."

"Who's going to do your face?" she said severely.

He parried it like a running back. "Jennifer ate my bear."

"You're going to eat this cake of soap if you don't wash pretty soon."

> More than meets the eyes,
> I don't bot stake paro judys . . .

He grabbed the cloth from her menacing hand and scrubbed it into his hair. Soapy water dribbled into his eyes. He considered screaming, then squeezed them shut until the stinging abated.

"Why didn't Jennifer stay with us?"

"Because you were fighting. Grandmommy Muriel took her home where she'd be safe."

"In the refrigerator?"

"Is that where she usually sleeps?"

"She hit me first. She ate my bear."

"There were plenty of bears. And I saw who hit who."

"Mommy puts her in the refrigerator."

"Wash. Just do your arms and hands and we can get out."
Muriel, Ed's mother, had previously reported the refrigerator
allegation. Why would the child say something like that? she
asked. Sandra had been in Columbia Presbyterian with number
three, a daughter as yet nameless. I presume you do know how to
stop, Margo said to her. Yes, Mother, since you ask. He's having a
vasectomy while I'm in the hospital. I hope it hurts a little,
Margo said. The son of a bitch sprays semen around like Agent
Orange. I wanted three, Sandra said.

Not a woman to put a child in the refrigerator. Only at
Margo and Muriel's united demand had she surrendered Eric and
Jennifer.

Margo lifted Eric out of the tub, set him onto the lavender
bath mat, stepped out herself, swaddled him in a bath towel.

Eric was the sensitive child. Jennifer was solid latex but
smart enough to practice strategic howling when Eric bashed her
one. Neither of them yet had demanded Mommy, even after five
days.

"Grandmommy Muriel will put Jennifer in the refrigerator,"
said Eric again.

"I'm going to put you in bed. That's what I'm going to do."

"No!" Double fortissimo.

"With me. I'll read and you can snuggle down with me until
Granddaddy comes home."

After an hour of wiggling and whining Eric abruptly ran
down and became adorable in sleep, the skin almost translucent

over delicate bones. His hair shone. When the phone rang he didn't wake.

It was Sandra, home two days with number three, still unnamed. She spoke of her as Baby with enthusiasm. Baby was a sweet, tractable child just as Eric had been.

"Do you want me to come up?" Margo asked loyally.

"No. Just give me three more days alone with this one. I'll be fine."

"I should be hovering. Muriel keeps reminding me."

"It's okay, Mother. I'm fine."

"I won't compete for Best Grandmother Award. She can have it. She has nothing else to do with her life."

"It's *okay,* Mother."

"I didn't ask to be a grandmother. You did this to me. I'm still a young and vital person."

"You're a kick, Mother. You couldn't wait to get all of us out of the house and you've been careening around like a handball ever since we left."

"That's not true. You were difficult teenagers. How did I know you were going to start having babies all over the place?"

"How's the painting going?"

"I placed two in the Prince William County show. Don't divert me while I'm feeling sorry for myself—by the way, have you been abusing the children?"

"For Christ's sake, Mother!"

"They haven't asked for you since they got here—"

"They're very secure. They love their grandmommies."

"—and Eric keeps saying you put Jennifer in the refrigerator. Muriel hints darkly that I've spawned a monster."

"That's a crazy cartoon he saw on the Monty Python show. They put this little girl into the refrigerator, and when they go to take her out she's turned into a gallon of milk. Eric's been after me to do it ever since."

"What's he doing watching Monty Python in the middle of the night?"

"Have you tried putting him to bed?"

"He's sleeping like an angel beside me right now."

"In his own bed, Mother! You're going to ruin him for me. I can't take three of them to bed. Besides, Ed carries him around the house like a football. They fall asleep on the couch with the TV on. It's like being mother of four."

Margo sighed. "Are you sure you don't want me to come up?"

"We'd be at each other's throats in a day. I'm grateful to you now. Let's leave it at that, okay?"

After they hung up Margo carried Eric to what had been Sandra's bedroom, propped pillows around him in case he should roll. Turned out lights. She went into what still occasionally was Libby's room, now Margo's art studio. The painting on the easel was her self-portrait, heavier than Margo, the eyes full of rage, the face garishly lighted against the purple shadows. It was titled *Menopause* and had been rejected from the show in favor of her two abstracts.

As she heard Henry's step on the porch she turned out the light. She had already determined not to discuss the hour of arrival. By the time he'd checked the mail she'd heated the decaf.

"Hello, Granddaddy," she said to his back.

Henry didn't flinch. They weren't his grandchildren. The four-deep adolescent years had inoculated him against generational sensitivities. "Hello Granddaddy" was a dart against the side of a trash compactor.

After the ten o'clock news on Channel 5, they watched a rerun of M*A*S*H while he ate an egg roll, shrimp-fried rice, and Buddhist Delight from a flowered paper plate on the coffee table. At 11:15 he raised his head.

"Is he crying?"

A minute later Margo was back, Eric coughing and flushed in her arms. "Burning up," she said, set him on Henry's lap, headed for the phone. Eric whined, twisting against Henry's chest, then coughed heavily, gasping for breath between spasms.

"He was fine," Margo said to Sandra. "Just a slight cold was all."

"You didn't tell me about the cold. My God, Mother."

"It wasn't that bad. Kids have colds."

"Well, you've got yourself a job now, Grandmommy. It's his asthmatic bronchitis. Is he hot? I'll bet it's 103 already. Start with half an aspirin and an alcohol rub for the fever. And steam. See if you can get his chest opened up. Run the shower in the bathroom. If that doesn't work you may have to get him to the emergency room for a shot. I just wish you'd told me."

"What difference would it have made?"

But even a small crisis was better than lassitude. Margo pushed Henry out in the direction of the all-night drug store for the Benadryl, headed for the bathroom with Eric, now at last whimpering for his Mommy.

In the end none of the expedients worked. At 1:30 Henry wound up in the windowless waiting room while Margo and the emergency crew ministered to Eric. At ten past two she appeared to report. Eric was finally asleep. If his breathing stayed clear they could take him home. Half an hour, maybe.

"She never mentioned asthmatic bronchitis," Margo said.

Henry was reading a copy of *Sports Illustrated* with the cover and table of contents missing. "Maybe it was a baby thing. Maybe she thought he was over it."

"If I'm supposed to play grandmother, it seems at least she could have started me with a full deck."

Henry snapped her a glance over the half-glasses. Up, down. Half a second. Eloquent after his fashion. The waiting room had one red vending machine for Coke and Dr. Pepper and a blue one with peanut-butter crackers, taco chips, and nothing else. There were molded plastic seats, orange along two walls and purple in the middle, back-to-back as in musical chairs. Two angry-looking black teenagers were lurking just outside the doorway, smoking in defiance of the posted regulation in the hallway, waiting for a third who had come in half an hour ago with scalp lacerations.

"He was fine when we were taking a bath," Margo said defensively.

"Who's 'we'? You and Eric?"

She saw it coming and declined to answer. He stared steadily at her over the glasses now, head tilted down, waiting. He would stare until she answered.

"What's wrong with that?"

He waited, meeting her eyes, not quite hostile. "Did you do that with Marty and Thomas, too?"

"The child is three years old, Henry. I didn't stimulate him, for God's sake. I just made him wash. Asthma isn't necessarily emotional. Don't try to lay that on me." Margo grabbed another tattered magazine to escape his eyes, flipped through the pages without looking at them. Then she put it down and stood over him, speaking quietly. "For ten years you've been laying trips on me, making me feel apologetic for my children, for my conspicuous inadequacies. My housekeeping. My absent financial contribution. With that look, Henry. Just the way your mother did it to you."

Henry sighed and concentrated on a story about a polo

match. There was a picture of a red-shirted rider laid across a chestnut horse galloping full out. The player was reaching over with his right arm to the horse's left for a backhand swing.

"And the sigh. Signifying my sharp tongue. My ultimate failing. Henry, I have had all I can stand of your everlasting patience. Starting tomorrow"—she sat down beside him, her mouth three inches from his ear, speaking very softly—"I want to resign from you, from grandmotherhood, from myself. I am resigning my role as cook, housekeeper, and chief klutz in your life. How much will you pay me to go?"

"Two hundred a week," he said promptly.

"You said three hundred before."

Henry closed his eyes. "How about four?"

Her eyes filled with tears. Despite all resolve she put a hand on his arm. "All I want is to be loved. To be important to someone. You, even."

"Okay."

"How can I be important to you? I'm pleading, Henry."

Henry put down the magazine. Stood. He put his arms around her and they rocked slowly, almost as though the Coke machine were a jukebox with Stevie Wonder singing "You Are the Sunshine of My Life."

# 10

---

Her name was E. Spalding Bruce. She had been riffed from one of the expiring children's programs and was therefore the mandatory selection to be Henry's assistant. He could take her or he could leave the slot vacant.

The summary list noted that she was single, thirty-one, had a B.A. in psychology from Denison and work experience going back only two years. Last hired, first fired. On the back of her Form 171 someone had penciled "Bright & competent, if not personable."

Henry's first reaction when she came for her interview was that she must be ill. She was dressed in a dark gray shapeless smock. Her hair was lifeless. Her posture was lifeless. She looks beaten, he thought. She didn't look thirty-one—she looked forty-five. Only her eyes were pretty—prominent, without cosmetics. Wary.

Henry had never developed a satisfactory job interview technique. If they were good they usually interviewed themselves without much prompting.

E. Spalding Bruce was shown into his office and seated herself without being bidden or offering her hand. Eye contact, sporadic. *Why is she so defensive if she knows we have to take her?*

Henry tried the only overture he could think of. "I went to Denison for a year—before the war."

She met his eye for a long moment but did not smile.

"I majored in psych, too."

She glanced at him again as though to see whether she were being baited. "Maybe there's hope for me, then." The voice had an edge to it, almost as though she were saying something sarcastic.

Henry remembered the poison pencil note on the back of her Form 171 and realized suddenly that she was not sure of being hired at all. Other offices could have decided to live with their vacancies rather than take her. It had been almost ten weeks since she had been dropped by the Children's Bureau.

"Why don't we do this procedure backward," he suggested. "Why don't I tell you now that we'll take you. Then we can go on with our interview more comfortably."

Another wary look, but her lips formed a soundless "thank you." She leaned back into the chair for a moment. Henry wondered if she might cry, then decided that this woman seldom cried.

They chatted a little. She lived in a basement efficiency near Crystal City. There was a child of five with her mother in Ohio. She'd worked three years after college for the Cleveland Foundation, then followed the child's father to Washington. The circumstances of arrivals and departures were shadows behind the one clear fact: this woman was alone. After she'd been riffed the unemployment money had taken six weeks to start and would run out too soon.

Henry pulled four ten dollar bills from his pocket. "Keep these until you get on your feet."

"Oh, I couldn't!" She stared at the little stack of bills on the desk as though it were about to explode. "You shouldn't do that. What if I never came back?"

"There's no hurry about repayment. You don't even have to owe it to me. It's my investment in the human race. Someday you can give it to somebody who needs it."

"You're terribly kind. I just couldn't." She was on her feet. Henry stood with her.

"It's up to you. Perhaps you could get something for your little girl."

"He's a boy." She was shaking her head, trembling as she stood.

"Maybe a hot meal for yourself. No obligation. Please understand."

Suddenly she grabbed the bills, stuffed them in her purse and rushed out the door. Then she was back. "When do I start?"

"Monday. We'll expedite, as we say in our native federal tongue."

When he smiled there was no returning smile. She nodded and disappeared.

Henry had been working for the government off and on for eighteen years. His title was always Acting Director. When the Democrats had come in they said "Do God's work." When the Republicans had come in they said "Save money." To Henry both had seemed laudable objectives. The Reagan administration wanted to do both as though to prove at last that each was unattainable. Henry was less disturbed by it than he would have been when he was younger. His repaired heart was holding up superbly. On good days his arthritis was minimal. He was still running most of a mile three or four times a week. It was April again. Baseball season would start in a matter of days.

His early nurturing had included the Red Sox, the Braves,

and peanut butter a long time before the Braves left Boston and peanut butter was homogenized. One of his earliest memories was of his father's taking him to a Braves game and afterward introducing him to Rabbit Maranville. Henry never played well enough to make a varsity team but he loved the game. He collected baseball cards and listened to Jim Britt narrate, inch by inch, the annual heartbreaking humiliation of the Red Sox by the Yankees. And through a lifetime of moderately successful careers as a teacher, social worker, administrator, and mediator there was a time each spring when he regretted that he had not committed himself to baseball, in some supporting capacity if not as a player, for no more reason than to hear the hallowed echoes of bats and mitts and to smell the mustard.

Each year he took a day's leave without telling Margo and drove to Baltimore for the pleasure of an Orioles game before the first of May.

He took E. Spalding Bruce to the 1984 game two days before she came to work for him. He was leaving the building to make his solitary annual pilgrimage when she accosted him on the sidewalk.

"Where are you going?" she demanded.

"Out to the ball game. Why?"

She scowled. "I didn't mean to ask you that. I only wanted to speak to you and you were getting away."

"It's okay."

She held out four ten-dollar bills. "A check came from my mother. I want to give this back to you."

Henry grinned at her. "Does this mean the end of everything so soon?" But she missed the smile.

"Oh, I'll be there Monday. I just couldn't—" she stopped.

"Couldn't what?"

"I just couldn't let myself. I had to bring it back."

"It's all right." Henry took the bills from her and jammed them into his pocket. "Come with me to the Orioles game. This will be my only trip this year. If you worked for me I couldn't ask you, but since we're just friends—acquaintances—I can ask and you can accept without discomfort. Of course if you wouldn't let me lend you forty dollars, you wouldn't let me take you to a baseball game, so I'm surely wasting my breath, but as a common courtesy—"

"You're weird. You know that, don't you."

Henry pursed his lips and thought about it. "Perverse, perhaps. I hadn't thought about weird."

She was amused. Not smiling. "I'll let you give me a ride to Baltimore. If I go to the ball game I'll pay my own way. I don't let men pick me up."

But she did sit with him and kept score with the stub of an old pencil. She knew more about baseball than he did. She was from Cleveland and the Orioles were playing the Indians—were creamed by the Indians. E. Spalding Bruce loved every minute of it and never smiled once.

"You know why I went with you?" she said on the way home. "You're the only one who didn't ask me what the E stands for."

"I presumed that if you liked it you'd be using it instead of Spalding. What do people call you?"

"Spalding."

Henry left her at a bus stop because she refused a ride home.

E. Spalding Bruce went about her duties in a manner that could only be described as efficient and morose. She never smiled, had no small talk for anyone. She arrived early, took a short lunch at her desk, worked late if there was the smallest reason to do so. The fact of their shared ball game had ceased to exist.

Henry's attempts to amuse her in small ways, to do anything to brighten that sad face, were never acknowledged and never rejected. Once he tried asking her about her son.

"I don't have a son."

"But you said—"

"I lied. My mother doesn't have him. He was put up for adoption."

"I'm sorry—" Henry felt as though he'd blundered into a swamp.

"Don't," she said. "Just please don't. I can't imagine what ever made me bring it up."

Watching her trudge through her days, Henry's heart ached. She seemed to be grimly treading water because the alternative was to drown. But she wouldn't let anyone help.

He couldn't get comfortable calling a young woman Spalding, though no one else in the office seemed to give it a second thought. One day he elided Spalding and Bruce into Spoose on a sheet of instructions for a position paper. Once again there was no acknowledgment.

Came six o'clock and she was still at her desk. Henry was the only other person left.

"Quit," he said, pulling on his coat. "Go home."

"I'm not finished." She didn't look up.

"Do you get enough to eat? Enough sleep?" he said. "Not that it's any of my business."

"That's right." Still no eye contact.

It was like offering a tidbit to an alley cat and getting scratched for your pains. The hell with her. He went out and shut the door.

．  ．  ．

The next morning she was missing, nor did she come in all day—uncharacteristic behavior. And conspicuous. Henry's division was housed in a rectangular suite of offices that he pictured as a frame of domesticated bees, with his own large office in one corner, his assistant in a small one adjacent, both opening onto a foyer for the secretary-receptionist and two chairs and a philodendron for guests. The secretary was an athletic-looking black woman named Barbara with a loud laugh and a nose for news. In an organization of twenty-two souls she was the gossip clearinghouse, very helpful to a reticent manager like Henry.

At three o'clock that afternoon Barbara presented herself at his desk.

"What do you think?" she said. "I've called her number three times. Nobody answers."

"Did she say anything to you yesterday?"

"Not a word."

"She looked terrible."

"She's looked terrible since she got here."

They arranged that Barbara should continue to call—from home that evening if necessary. Barbara thought she didn't have a boyfriend. "I just picture her crawling into her mouse hole and dying every night."

The next morning Barbara came in worried. "I went to her place last night and got her landlord to let me look in her room. She hasn't been there for at least a day. Her cat was ready to eat the furniture."

At two the second afternoon word came from City Hospital. She'd been picked up on the Mall in a diabetic coma, near death. It had taken thirty-six hours to get a coherent statement from her.

"Did she know she was diabetic?" Barbara asked.

"I don't think so."

"Well, no wonder."

It was the beginning of a rebirth for E. Spalding Bruce. No less than ten of the office people, including Henry and Barbara, crowded into her hospital room to find her, huge-eyed, in an ugly johnny with an IV running into her wrist.

"Good God!" was all she could say. She still wouldn't cry.

They gave her a whole horseshoe of flowers with SPOOSE on it in big silver letters.

"We got it cheap from a funeral parlor," said Billy from the administration group. She nearly laughed and cried at the same time.

It took two weeks to get her back. She'd run her batteries flat. She came in on a Wednesday morning and had opened Henry's mail and drafted four responses for his signature by the time he arrived.

"Who watered the philodendron while I was gone?" she growled. "This place doesn't deserve plants."

She looked like a crocus in March—a new bit of color in her cheeks, hair clean and soft, eyes enormous. Henry considered hugging her. "How do you feel?" was what he said.

"You wouldn't believe the difference. I actually looked forward to coming in today." Now she was not looking at him again.

"It's a good bunch of people here."

"Something like that." Busy sorting through unanswered reports on his credenza. Back turned to him. "I got hugged by thirteen people when I walked in here."

"I almost hugged you, too."

"You'd have ruptured yourself," she said over her shoulder, leaving fast.

*Now what the hell did that mean?* Henry frowned. He realized she'd left a hint of cologne in her wake.

The difference in her during the weeks that followed continued to amaze him. She kept her grump in place, but now she was full of energy, not only with Henry's work load, but lending a hand to anyone who could use it. Drawing on her past experience with private foundations, she drafted a handbook for grantees that she called *Life after Uncle* that detailed strategies for development of community and foundation support as government moneys were phasing out. Henry was so pleased with it that he went to see Billy about getting an award for her.

"You'll get a kick out of this," Billy told him. "She's been worrying about your image in the office. She's trying to be sure we understand you."

Henry smiled uncomfortably.

"Don't knock it. It could be the other way around too easy. Have you ever seen such a changed person? Did you know she's pitching for the softball team now?"

Henry hadn't known. "What softball team?" he asked E. Spalding Bruce later.

"I'm going to deny you asked me that."

"You mean I should have known."

"I mean you should have been out rooting for them all these years."

"Nobody asked me."

"Nobody knew you liked baseball."

"Did you tell them?"

"You think I'm crazy?"

"I didn't mean about the game we saw."

"I don't know what you're talking about," she snapped.

As usual, Henry said nothing—at least until the end of the day when she stopped back to say good night.

"Billy said you've been worrying about my image with staff," he said. "I was under the impression I had good staff relations. In fact I've rather prided myself on it."

"They think you're God—loving in a remote sort of way."

"What do you think?"

"I don't have to answer that," she said crossly and started to leave.

"Why not?"

"Because you've got a wife and four kids and you're my boss and I'm too stupid to be alive. Now will you leave me the hell alone?" She was standing in the doorway glaring at him. When he rose from his chair she fled.

The next Wednesday after work Henry followed a scrawled set of directions to a playing area off the Mall—one of dozens, he discovered. At first everyone in each of them seemed to be wearing red shirts and white shorts or white shirts and red shorts. Some had red coolers for beer, some white—and some red, white, and blue. On a hot June evening it looked like a national Sunday school picnic with Henry as minister in his dark suit and gray tie wandering among the parishioners—on a hot June evening faintly scented of river, of oaks and maples and willows, of the last fumes of the echoing traffic across the Roosevelt Bridge. There was an explosion of motion and noise to Henry's left as a burly black man smashed a long drive and leaped around the basepaths. To the right in another backed-up playing area a lone, bored, left-fielding girl in raspberry shorts danced to a tune audible only inside her head. Henry moved on, searching for a familiar face.

They saw him first, hailed him over, shoved a beer into his hand, offered chips, nachos, a corner of a plaid blanket to sit on — Billy, Barbara, Ray with wife and baby, Fred, a dozen more from other floors whom Henry might have seen on the elevator, and E. Spalding Bruce, sweet as a birch tree. She went to bat, left-handed, hit a grounder to short, got thrown out at first. Henry stood to speak to her as she returned. "Who's ahead?"

"Us," she said, looking smug. "Twelve to ten." Henry became aware without knowing how that Billy and Ray were smoking dope and considering offering some to him.

"Would you like to get a bite later?" he said quietly.

She took so long to respond that Henry thought she might not have heard. Finally she asked where his car was ("Don't point") and instructed him to go there at the start of the seventh inning, which would be the last. ("You'll have done your fatherly duty.")

Two hours later they sat across a small table in the Alexandria Hojo's ("No one local comes in here"), having consumed clam chowder and side orders of coleslaw, she still in T-shirt and shorts, he tie-less, sleeves rolled ("so you don't look like my pimp").

"What do we do about this?" Henry asked her.

Another long silence, not reticence but thinking, playing out the knights and bishops. "Whatever we have to do," she said finally, "when there's no choice."

"I'll never do anything to hurt Margo."

"You already have."

"What are you talking about? I've never touched you."

"What difference does that make?"

"But I haven't done anything. Am I to blame for what I feel?"

"No, that's a given. But that's what will hurt her."

"How will she know?"

"She'll know."

It took a while. At first Margo was too busy with her own existence to notice. When she did sense something it took a long time to surface. It came after a Friday night's uninspired loving.

"What's happened to us, Henry?"

"Nothing. I'm just tired."

"Tired of me?"

"Of course not."

"Where do you go nights when you come home late?"

"Sometimes work. Sometimes softball games."

"Do you have someone else?"

"No."

This was an unstable time for Margo. Only Libby was home from time to time. Thomas was away at VMI. Marty was God knows where, and Sandra was married in New York with her three babies. Grandmotherhood and hot flashes were more than she could bear. Now this, whatever it was.

"Softball? You're playing softball?"

"I root for our team. Maybe they'll let me play later on."

With frightening clairvoyance Margo said, "Who do you play with, the pitcher?"

No, goddammit, Henry didn't play with anyone and he would not listen to this sort of rubbish, he said, staying and listening to it.

"Do you realize what a pushover you are for women? What a child in a candy shop you are? Have you ever had a woman who didn't come after you first? I'm your third wife, Henry. Is the day coming when I'll find a note in the kitchen: 'Time for a change'?"

Henry lied poorly, losing track of the line where truth ended. Nothing had happened between him and his Spoose beyond evenings of chowder and coleslaw. Nothing except longing. She wouldn't let him go to her apartment because they would fall into bed and it would be a disaster when they were heard. She was a noisy lover, she said. Security was always her first concern. She couldn't bear it if the office knew, and it would be bad for him, as he should know if he had any sense. "If we're going to make love, it will have to be premeditated. We'll have to find a hotel or go away where no one knows us."

Besides, she didn't want to make love because she might want to keep him. She didn't dare make love to someone she loved. She said this.

Shortly afterward she said she always had affairs with married men because it was a guarantee against emotional entanglements.

Shortly after that she said she was cursed with a proclivity to fall in love only with those who were legally unavailable to her.

Henry was by this time able to accept such inconsistencies even though he couldn't make them add up. If he had wisdom, it was in not trying and in keeping his observations to himself.

"Do you know why I fell in love with you?" she said.

"Because I didn't ask what the E meant."

No — not that, although it was nice, as were the loan of the forty dollars and the gift of her nickname and the delegation to her hospital room. What then? It was the way his hair curled at the back of his neck. It made her want to kiss it.

Literally? Well, yes.

Why hadn't she done it? Why didn't she do it now? They

were sitting in his steamed-up TR6 in a July thunderstorm that had ruined a softball game.

So she did lean to kiss the back of his neck, and somehow the electricity of it turned his body to face her, and the intensity of their first embrace left them both shaken, gasping for completion, thwarted only by the design of a British sports car.

"I don't understand it," he said, anchored in his bucket seat, staring straight ahead. "I'm sixty years old, I love my wife and my home and will never leave them, but when we touch each other there's something happens that never happened before."

"It's a gift."

"You felt it, too?"

"Oh yes. I had a little climax."

"From a kiss? Do you always do that?"

"I never have before."

On the way home Henry considered this piece of intelligence with a more analytical mind than a man in love would have wished. He had a habit of placing a percentage value on the statements of those whom he met in his Washington and Fauquier County days and nights, perhaps acquired from a decade of attempting to raise adolescents and a lifetime of trying not to love too many women. When Thomas denied knowledge of the death of the microwave oven, Henry's cerebral scanner rang a faint 42 percent. When Margo denied the same knowledge a 95 percent registered.

When E. Spalding Bruce had said she was a noisy lover it won a hopeful 67 percent, pending verification. A climax with a first kiss, however passionate, rated only an irresolute 22 percent—although it had been a lovely thing for her to say.

Not long after Henry arrived home Margo tuned in to his wave length. Henry saw it happen, as though a January wind had suddenly burst in through the kitchen door. She stopped eating and stared at him, holding back tears.

"Baseball," he said. "Softball, rather."

"Sure."

"There was a thunderstorm, so I quit and came home."

"Sure."

"Your lips tell me yes, yes, but there's no, no in your eyes."

"It isn't funny, Henry." The tears came now. Silently.

"Come on, Margo. What is it tonight?"

"You've become a dead person. You never look me in the eye any more—"

Henry looked at her dead in the eye.

"—unless I point it out. We almost never make love—"

"Last Saturday."

"—except Saturdays. There was a time you couldn't keep your hands off me, when I couldn't get you off the phone, when you hurried home, when you took me everywhere—"

"You want to come to a softball game? Come in with me next Thursday, do the museums. I'll take you to the Flagship for lunch, and we'll watch the softball game after work."

Margo just looked at him. Then she assailed him by assailing herself. She wasn't good enough for him, she said. Her body was aging, her spirit depleted. He had nothing left for her but silent judgment, just as he had judged her children one after another.

Henry could not meet this attack, and since there was no place to run he withdrew his head, legs, and tail and turned off his hearing while she beat on his shell—and thereby he demonstrated his role as failed lover because he wouldn't fight.

The next Thursday when Margo chose not to come to Washington, Henry exhumed the baseball glove Thomas had given him, borrowed one of Thomas' Rugby shirts, and wore it and his sneakers with his suit trousers to that evening's game.

The palpable lack of enthusiasm upon his arrival thus attired should have told him he'd stepped out of role, but he was too absorbed in his own needs to see. For the past several weeks he had been intermixing sprinting with his jogging, to be sure there wouldn't be embarrassing leg cramps halfway down the base path to first. For the time being his arthritis was in almost total remission, too. If he was going to grace the team with the presence of a sexagenarian infielder, now was the time to do it.

Game time was still half an hour away, allowing for a little informal batting practice. Henry joined the clutch of players in the infield, retrieved but did not correctly charge a slow-rolling ground ball, wound up playing catch with Billy and Ray. Billy dropped out for a turn at bat and after five minutes offered Henry a chance. It was not because he'd earned the right to be there, and in his awareness he felt compelled to swing for the outfield. He would have stood on his head to be accepted.

E. Spalding Bruce took the pitcher's mound and lobbed an easy one to him, inside, belt-high. In his entire life he had never conquered the inside pitch. He chopped at it and drove it into home plate. He could almost feel the onlookers turning away. The next pitch was a fat one, a little outside, a little low, a gift from God or Spoose. Henry's roundhouse swing drove it six feet over the head of the left fielder with a slap that stopped conversation.

Wise enough to quit while he was ahead, Henry handed the bat to Ray and went to sit on his glove beside Billy, realizing too late that Billy was dragging on a roach that had been passing quietly among a circle of players. Without a word Billy handed it to Henry, who had not been within a hundred feet of marijuana since his disastrous affair with Helen of Missouri.

He took the stub, which wasn't more than a quarter inch long, juggled it to his lips, inhaled deeply, burned both his fingers and his mouth, and dropped it in the sand.

"That's okay," Billy said quickly. "Just step on it without being conspicuous. Some plainclothes guys are coming up on third base."

Henry closed his eyes and dropped his head in an inadvertent effort to make himself disappear—and because the pot was nothing like the mild weeds Helen had given him. This stuff made him instantly drunk—stupefied, as though he'd belted down a tray of double martinis. When the police came closer he felt as though he'd been painted orange and set on a throne. Only when he heard the game starting could he recover enough to open his eyes.

By the third inning he'd come down sufficiently to ask Billy if there was a chance he could get into the game for an inning or two.

"Maybe if we're ahead," Billy said reluctantly.

There was still time to back off but Henry would have none of it. He watched while Billy went to Miles Johnson, the long-suffering, kindly, emaciated manager—for better or worse, not from Henry's office—to petition on Henry's behalf, not because he had earned it but because he was pulling rank. All this was clearly readable in the look Miles shot Henry over Billy's shoulder—the sort of look Henry was so good at shooting himself, at undeserving adolescents, at ill-mannered motorists and jay-walking pedestrians—and wives.

Still Henry sat on his glove, visibly hopeful, buoyed by the remnants of a lungful of high-quality Afghan hashish, until finally in the bottom of the sixth Miles Johnson looked at him again and said, "You're batting next."

This was a team big on chatter. Give 'em hell, Henry. Let's get a rally going, Henry. One out, nobody on. The opposing pitcher, who looked younger than Henry's Libby, opened with a toss that took a trajectory like a mortar shell, a high lob that plopped to the ground two feet behind the plate.

*Way to go, Henry. Look 'em over, baby.*

The second pitch was like the first.

*Wait 'em out, baby.*

There was no umpire to call balls and strikes. The pitcher simply kept tossing in bombs until the batter would be embarrassed into swinging, which is what Henry did on the third pitch, slapping it on one bounce to the shortstop, who threw him out handily at first.

*Good try, Henry. Wait till next time.*

If he'd had a choice he'd have ducked out with that, but the next batter flied to left and Henry was sent to second base. He trotted to the field with a case of the shakes that no sexagenarian should feel, short of being cornered after spying for the People's Republic of China. Suddenly he was a fourteen-year-old boy with a cracking voice praying that no ground ball would come his way. But God spared him not. The first hit was a grass cutter that a superb infielder could have stopped but it snaked by him for a single.

*Nice try, Henry.*

The second hit was well over his head, with the shortstop (a woman) taking no chances, covering second base for the throw-in that was too late in any event.

Tying run on first. Go-ahead run at the plate. Tension on the base paths. Opposing batter, Henry half-overheard, was a Sal Pandemonium. He looked like a Greek Ted Williams. On the first pitch he hit a line drive well over Henry's head, and in the ensuing melee of galloping and yelling Henry did his best to keep out of the way—but, alas, not well enough. As he stood watching the slugger race toward third base, something thumped Henry hard in the back—a thrown softball—the heave-in toward home plate to cut off the leading run that scored easily by the time the ball was retrieved and relayed.

"For God's sake," came a scream from right field. "If you can't play ball, at least keep out of the way."

When he got to the car, E. Spalding Bruce was there waiting. It was nearly dark.

"Where have you been?"

"I took a long walk."

"You should have stayed. Mike hit a triple with two on. He was terribly embarrassed to have yelled at you like that. He forgets it's just a game."

"Yeah—so do I."

She looked at him with a mixture of tenderness and annoyance. "It's not the end of your life, you know. Next time you'll do better."

"There won't be a next time."

"Come on, Henry. I won't let you have a stupid softball game symbolizing the end of your manhood."

"I couldn't have put it better myself."

She took his hand and carefully bit the knuckle of his forefinger, then kissed it. "Come home with me."

"You said we couldn't at your place. We have to premeditate."

"I've premeditated. My landlord's away. No one to hear us. I just hadn't had a chance to tell you."

.    .    .

All through the spring her insistence on security had been as elaborate as something out of John le Carré. Absolutely no warmth or other impropriety at the office, no lunches together, no meetings after work except after softball, and these only with utmost discretion.

Her apartment was hardly more than a single basement room in a quaint neighborhood of 1920s houses across the Jefferson Davis Highway from Crystal City. You parked on Twentieth Street, walked through the driveway around to the private entrance in full view of the landlord above and the kitchen window of the lady next door. Another reason she'd kept him away — until now.

Henry's fears for his manhood were quickly dissolved in the wild lovemaking that startled them both.

"You're really something," she said finally.

"I was responding to you. I'm very sensitive to sounds like that."

"You see why I had to have privacy?"

Her eyes fell to his scar, her fingers traced its line down his chest. "I love this," she said. "It's kept you alive for me."

"Don't." He shook his head. The pouting, jagged tissue still seemed ugly to his eyes even after three years.

"Why?" She tried to kiss it, but he flinched involuntarily. She looked at him almost in surprise.

"I'm sorry. I can't help it," he said.

"You could."

But she was wrong. He couldn't even play softball. He felt suddenly absurd. He was in bed with the wrong generation.

.    .    .

*What will change now?* Henry thought on his drive home. He planned and executed a self-deprecating recital of his fiasco at second base as a magnetic shield to block Margo's intuitional probing and went to bed exhausted. When she crawled in with him he clamped her body to his as he had not done in years.

Without realizing it he slept. He was back at Denison cutting classes. Tomorrow he had a final exam in history. He studied hopelessly, unable to cram four months into two hours. He wandered out onto the campus, struggling to cover his naked body with a gym towel.

He woke in a sweat. His hair was drenched, and the pillow, too. He was alone in bed. From down the hallway came dim light.

Margo was on the couch, sitting upright staring at the black television tube. She was wrapped in the housecoat she'd worn to paint the kitchen. Besides the paint stains one sleeve was discolored by a coffee spill. The other sleeve was ripped under the arm. When Henry came to sit beside her she closed her eyes. Her back stiffened. The cords in her neck were trembling. She was bracing herself as though he were going to hit her. He tried to take her hand but she clutched it to her side.

"What's wrong with me?" she said finally. Eyes still closed.

"Nothing. Come back to bed. Let me hold you."

"I want to know what's wrong with me. I want to know what she does for you that I can't do. Is she young, Henry?" She looked at him now. Her eyes were holes in her face. In pain her beauty deserted her.

"There isn't any she."

"Look me in the eye and say it."

He looked her in the eye and said it, but she turned away.

"You're not the sort of man who should be having affairs. You fall in love with everyone you touch."

"I'm not touching anybody, Margo. Come back to bed."

She searched his face again. "How many women have you taken to bed without falling in love with them?"

"Come back to bed, sweetie. I've got to work tomorrow."

"You said you'd give me four hundred a week. Do you want to get rid of me that badly?"

"For Christ's sake, Margo!" He tried to take her arm again, but she wrenched away from him.

"Go to bed yourself! Sleep! I'm not stopping you!"

He rose and stood over her. What he saw in her face now was terror. With a great sigh he turned away and went toward the bedroom.

"If you leave me, Henry, I will be your enemy!" The sound of her cry rang down the hallway after him.


At work E. Spalding Bruce was even more remote than usual. It was almost lunchtime before they could speak alone in his office.

"You look awful," she told him.

"Bad night."

"Trouble?"

"We need to talk."

"This is not the place."

"No one can hear us."

She turned to leave.

"Where then?" he said.

"Hojo's, tonight."

"I can't stay late."

"For lunch, then."

She wouldn't go in his car. She would catch a taxi. Her body was as rigid as Margo's had been. All Henry needed was two women drowning in pain.

She was ahead of him at the restaurant with a cup of coffee in front of her. She would accept no food. "What happened?"

A heavy motherly lady looking uncomfortable in a Hojo uniform stood at the booth. "I am Grace-your-Server today," she announced without meeting any eyes. "Would you like a drink before your meal? A menu?"

Henry knew the menu by heart. He ordered clam chowder and a salad, tried again to order for Spoose without success.

"What happened?" she repeated when Grace-your-Server had gone.

"Margo knows."

E. Spalding Bruce looked as though something had attacked her nostrils. "You *told* her?"

"Certainly not. She just can tell."

"What do you want to do?"

"I can't hurt my family."

She looked down into her lap, then back into his face. "You don't have to give them up to have me."

A last petition. Henry shoved a knife through it, being kind. "It isn't that I don't care about you."

"Don't give me that!"

"Please—don't get mad about it."

"And don't tell me when to get mad!"

*Nice try, Henry . . . Keep on swinging, Henry . . . . For God's sake, if you can't play ball, at least keep out of the way!*

"I can't go on lying to her," he said after a minute.

She shrugged. She almost smiled. "Well, it's the only way we can be together if you don't want to leave home."

Henry shook his head, opened his mouth, and closed it again in preference to repeating something inane. He had swallowed one mouthful of chowder.

"What's all this about lying? Telling nothing but the truth is for little kids and the Boy Scouts. The big lie is to say we never lie."

Henry looked at his dish.

"What it comes to," she said, "is you do what you have to do. I can't blame you for that."

Henry was still silent. Nothing could be said to make it better.

"I told you before—I have a talent for picking men who are totally inaccessible."

She waited. Then drank the cold coffee in one gulp, feeling on the seat for her purse. "I guess it's finally time for me to run away with the circus."

"I can't ask you to give up your job."

"I'm not doing it because you asked! Why do you think I'm mad! I refuse to suffer for you, Henry Calef!" She started to get up, sat back, chin in hand staring at him, shaking her head. "You do try to be a good person."

"I am a self-righteous man." *I am a rotten man. I can't help myself.*

"That's not true. If it were, I'd be the first to let you know." He tried to speak but she went on. "All I was saying is that you are a decent man. You think about doing the right thing."

"*You* don't? You of all people?"

"Not like you do. I do what I have to do. That's it."

"So what's the difference?"

"I don't suffer over it. When I lose the game I pick up my stuff and go home. I'm beaten. I hate it. I'll be back again, in some game, somewhere." She was holding her purse in her lap as though it were her softball glove. She shrugged. "That's it. I lose. I got into the wrong game. See you around someday."

"And that isn't ethics?"

"Not really. I'd take you away from her if I could."

He watched as she pushed out of the booth, strode across toward the exit, changed her mind, went to the rest room. Two minutes later she was back, looking down at him.

"Two afterthoughts," she said. "One: I can't just disappear overnight."

"Of course not. I'll help you find—"

"Two: You need to think about what it is in your marriage that made you come to me."

She refused a ride back to work. She would find a cab.

In time Grace-your-Server came with the check. Henry left a five-dollar tip on a five-dollar tab. Somebody had to feel good about this day.

He phoned the office to say he'd be late, then drove slowly southward along the parkway toward Mount Vernon. The Potomac on his left felt like New Hampshire. Finally he pulled into a recreational area where the river was wide enough that he could pretend it was a lake. The only other car was an old Pontiac Catalina with a retired couple—he dozing, she reading with her sun-shields flipped up from her glasses. Henry parked as far as possible from them. He left the car and climbed down to the water's edge and sat on a heavy fallen tree with silver-green moss on its sides.

There was, goddamm it, nothing wrong in his marriage. If he said it often enough it would be true. He loved Margo, who was, goddamm it, a decent human being.

He closed his eyes and saw E. Spalding Bruce walk painfully away from the Hojo's booth, make the turn, and disappear through the door.

So in the end his gift to her had been pain, as it had been to Margo. He could no longer blind himself to his self-indulgence with younger women, whether or not he took them to bed—for whatever excusable reasons. My God, what reasons could there be? That he couldn't resist a waif? Someone in need? Was that what had drawn him to Margo? When she'd suggested it was pity he'd denied it.

It was all a little too nice: warm-hearted Henry rescuing damsels. But now here came Henry the philanderer hanging them out to dry. Was he still too immature at sixty to take on family responsibility?

Or was he running from advancing age? The standard deviation, he thought, grimacing at his own wordplay.

A crow called four times in the trees behind him. Henry had loved crows from childhood when their cawing had meant summer release, the aroma of hot grass in the meadows above Center Harbor, the glint through the trees of blue lake water dancing in the sunlight, the feel under his bare feet of the weathered boards of the dock where the rowboat was anchored. Henry alone at dawn in the boat half a mile offshore, the water like steamed glass. Henry alone.

Finally he drove home. The house was empty at mid-afternoon. Margo's car was gone. He sat in her chair at the kitchen table and waited. He thought of going upstairs to see if her clothes had been moved, then restrained himself. There was a Land's End catalog on the table but he couldn't even concentrate on the ad copy. Finally when he heard her tires in the gravel he felt himself draw a great breath, as though he hadn't breathed since he'd come in and found her gone. He thought of going to hold her, remembered last night, stayed put.

She bustled in with two bags of groceries and dumped them onto the counter.

"Let me tell you something, buster!" she said without looking at him, taking out cans and jars, thumping them into the cupboards. "I've begged my last beg and shed my last tear. No punk like you is going to put me through a strainer. You're coming or you're going, but you can't have it both ways. I'm not going to stand guard over you. I don't want to follow you around with a rolled-up newspaper trying to catch you messing on the floor. I want you housebroken."

She looked at him over her glasses. One second. The Henry Calef look.

"You have a right to be angry," he said and realized it was relief he felt because he could respond to anger. It was her pain that paralyzed him.

"You're goddamned right I have a right."

"Even if it was nothing but the softball games."

"Whatever the games were, I don't want any more of them."

"Whatever they were will never happen again."

She stopped banging cans and searched his face.

"This is a recommitment, Margo. I really do love you. I have never not loved you. I'm here to suggest we go away together for a few days. Let's start all over. Where would you like to go?" He stood and held her to hide his tears in her hair.

It took her several minutes to respond. "You pick" was what she said.

# PART
# III

# 11

## 1. Libby

Libby had never been able to bear being wrong. She couldn't concede defeat even when all the evidence was against her. She would argue, sulk, lie. This drove Thomas to incredulous outrage. It turned the role of parent into a game of psychological hide-and-seek.

When in sixth grade she had been banished from the school bus for fighting, she first refused to admit it, then blamed the driver, finally said she'd held three boys at bay with her lunchbox. When witnesses swore the combatants had been Libby and a black girl (who was also banished), Libby insisted they were all lying, then said the other girl had called Thomas a hankie. She'd never heard of *honkey* but she knew it was an insult.

She and Thomas teased each other, belittled whatever the other said, betrayed minor confidences, raised embarrassment to an art form—and formed an iron alliance against the outer world. Even against parents when the stakes were high.

Because Libby had arrived as a petted only child there had been an unspoken agreement not to give her special breaks.

When the haying crew formed up she had been expected to lift or drag a forty-pound bale like all the others. She had driven the pick-up truck in the pasture when she had been too small to see where she was going; at the barns she had hauled water in the big blue pails, mucked out stalls, fought chickens for their eggs, sat vigil with expectant mares through filthy rainy cold April nights.

Her response had always been to outdo the others, to be superwoman, to put Thomas to shame if possible. If he had put off cutting the lawn she'd haul out the mower in a show of conspicuous virtue and hack away with it, while he ignored her or laughed at her, feigning no remorse.

Her approach to a task was often wildly eccentric. While it didn't matter if she mowed the grass in figure eights or trapezoids, it mattered a great deal if she fed the horses incorrectly or left the feed-room door open so they could push their way in and gorge themselves, possibly unto death.

But when she'd made mistakes, she found reproof unbearable. She couldn't admit error. She would deny the facts, blame someone else, lie in the face of overwhelming evidence. And she was a terrible liar.

"Did you vacuum your room, Libby?"

"Yes!"

"Then what are all these crumbs by your bed?"

"There aren't any crumbs!"

"Look—right there."

"Those aren't my crumbs."

"That's not the point. You said you'd vacuumed them up."

"I did!"

"Today?"

"Yes!"

The crumbs had been placed there by unseen enemies, by Soviet agents, by immaculate conception. Libby wouldn't quit.

"Why don't you just say you're sorry? Then it'll all be over."

"Because it wasn't my fault!"

In so many other ways she was an easy kid that her lying was almost an amusing quirk. At ten it had mattered less than it did at fifteen, when jeans and flannel shirts no longer hid her beauty. Her word was undependable; could she be allowed to attend football games?

"I'll look out for her," said Thomas.

Permission was reluctantly granted.

Then she wanted to become a cheerleader. That meant going to Graves Mountain Lodge for two weeks of intensive pre-season drill. Sandra had gone the year before. But Sandra was the truth-teller—she overwhelmed them with her truths.

"I tell the truth," Libby protested.

"Not often enough."

"When did I last—"

"This morning. You said you'd hung up your towel."

"I forgot."

It was rumored that two of the cheerleaders had smoked dope at camp last year. Could Libby be trusted?

"She wouldn't dare," said Thomas.

"Why not? She dares to do everything else."

"Because she knows I would kill her."

Libby went to the Episcopal chapel with whatever elements of the family were Episcopalians at the time. To Thomas' outrage she took Communion without having been confirmed. He told his parents. He threatened to tell the priest. Libby continued to take Communion.

Thomas defended her virtue in the locker room to the point of telling other players to leave his sister the hell alone, which had the effect of reducing Libby's potential supply of boy-friends to musicians and church-goers, all too shy to ask her out.

Fortunately, Libby's life was still filled with horses and pony club competitions—and family. She was the most family-minded member of a close-knit clan bonded by traditions like cutting a Christmas tree in the woods, hauling it home and frosting it with trimmings; carving pumpkins; hand-making valentines; celebrating all possible holidays; giving gifts on all possible occasions, including when someone was sick or hurt. The other children were frequently content to let Margo buy things for them to give one another. Libby selected her own presents and paid for them out of her limited resources—strange, improbable things at first, but in surprisingly good taste as she matured.

Then, when Libby was fifteen, Margo discovered she had stolen some of her Christmas money from another girl's purse. The pattern of lying had extended beyond home. The school handled it with discretion and firmness. Libby must go for counseling.

So she was ferried to the psychologist at Family Guidance for sessions first with Margo, then with Henry. Her history was analyzed. Libby listened but did not participate. Whatever she felt, the psychologist never got it out of her. She stopped stealing, but she still lied.

She and Thomas still fought, but they became closer than ever. When he went off to Virginia Military Institute, it was Libby he called collect to talk to, to get caught up on the news—and to argue with. Henry and Margo marveled in silence.

One epic weekend Thomas found himself stranded in Washington by a faithless girl who had promised to take him back to VMI by four o'clock Sunday afternoon. Dire consequences threatened. He had been late twice before. Henry and Margo were away. Only Libby could rescue him. Only the forbidden TR6 was available and in working condition.

But Libby had no license. Libby had never driven anything but the truck, with its automatic transmission, in an open field.

"I'll *teach* you how," Thomas said.

"On the phone? Thomas, you're crazy. Why don't you hitch-hike?"

"I can't."

"Why?"

"I always get picked up by fruits. C'mon, Libby. This is a matter of life and death."

Libby was accustomed to hyperbole, but she was weakening. "What, really?" she said.

"It depends. I could even get kicked out." There was silence. Thomas waited.

"What do I have to do?" she said finally.

"Do you know where he hides the key?"

"Of course." Libby knew every secret in the house, including the whereabouts of Thomas' *Hustler* collection.

"Okay. Get a pencil. You have to write down every step or you'll forget it."

Thomas slowly dictated.

"Insert key," she wrote. "Pull out choke (at right). Make sure shift is in nutril. Clutch left. Break right. Hand break doesn't hold."

He gave her precise directions to Washington National Airport, the only landmark Libby was remotely likely to find.

They allowed half an hour for her to experiment with shifting in the driveway. "Clutch catches near floor," read her notes. How had Thomas known that?

Additional problems—little gas and less money. Libby borrowed a credit card of Henry's from his bureau drawer. Unfortunately the card she took was for a clothing store. So she simply drove into the Citgo station, filled up with regular, and drove away without looking back. But she nearly hit the pump coming in, and the car bucked, jerked and stalled twice going out. Another customer stared and noted her license number, which he shared with the irate cashier.

Damn kids today. They're all high on drugs.

Out of her inexperience with sports cars Libby confused the tachometer with the speedometer. She told Thomas later that it *had* seemed strange to fly past all the other cars at only forty miles per hour.

The state trooper informed her she'd been driving twice that fast. She never could quite reconstruct what she told him. Something like an imminent death in the family, requiring her to rush to the airport to bring her father home. Accompanied by tears. Purse with license had been left on the dresser at home, of course.

Moved by compassion or suspicion, the trooper led Libby to the airport to help her find her father. She seriously thought of flying into the arms of the first fatherly stranger she found in the parking area, but Thomas blew her story before he realized she was under escort.

At least Thomas was able to drive away legally, but Libby received a citation and a summons to appear in court. She and Thomas spent the three-hour drive to VMI discussing strategies to avoid having to confess to Henry.

Thomas bought her exactly enough gas to get home and

showed her how to work the headlights and dimmer. The dimmer was important. Cops would think you were a drunk if you didn't dip your lights.

But Libby got lost.

She drove north on Interstate 81 as far as West Virginia before she realized she'd missed her exit. She was low on gas by then, so she had to steal from another Citgo station.

Margo covered for her, paid the Citgo stations, went to court with her, supervised her probationary year. They finally had to confess to Henry when it was time for her to get her driver's license. At least she'd been brand-loyal, Henry observed. When her probation was up he helped her to buy an old Dodge Dart, unlovely but dependable. He encouraged her to take a job at Burger King on the Warrenton bypass.

Then she began coming home late, ostensibly because of the midnight closing and subsequent cleanup chores, but she was surly when questioned. It was almost like her childhood pattern of working up to a spanking.

One night when she was still not home by midnight. Henry phoned the restaurant. Libby had left at eleven, the manager said.

One o'clock became two, then three, while Henry waited in the living room, more frightened and angry with each passing moment. At five minutes of four he heard faint sounds of tires on gravel. She'd killed the lights. She was walking on the grass. But there he was—angry father waiting up in an undershirt and jeans.

"Where in God's name have you been!" he bellowed.

At first she couldn't answer, dumbstruck to see him blocking the path to her bedroom. She looked haggard. Henry assumed it was booze. He couldn't bring himself to consider other substances.

"What kind of person are you becoming!"

"We had to stay to clean up. I didn't get out till almost one-thirty."

"You're lying, Libby. I talked to your manager. You left at eleven."

"I was still there. He just didn't see me." She didn't look as though she believed it herself. "And on the way home I had a flat tire."

"Come on, Libby. That story died before I was driving."

"Well, it's true."

Henry moved toward the door. "Give me your keys. I'm going to check the tire in your trunk."

Libby slumped into Henry's armchair. "There wasn't any flat." Henry realized abruptly that her shrill little girl voice was gone. This was a woman talking.

"Where were you, Libby?"

"With some girls. We stopped at Becky's apartment for a drink."

"Five hours for one drink? Girls only? Give me a break, Libby."

"There weren't any boys. . . ." She was struggling to keep her eyes open.

"Go to bed," Henry told her. "At a minimum this is the end of your job. And it's the end of your car until I see a few signs of maturity. At this point the best I can say is that I'm relieved you got home in one piece."

"You've got to make her stop lying," Margo said. "That's the one thing I can't stand."

"I've got to do it, huh? Just like that."

"Have you ever sat down and told her lying is wrong? I'm always the one. You've got to warn her she won't have a friend left in the world. You have to, Henry."

"It seems to me that her friends are too solid, if anything. They're a bulwark against us. What can I possibly say at this point to make her stop lying?"

"Sometimes there's nothing like a dose of old-fashioned morality."

Henry lay awake after Margo had fallen asleep. No magic formula came to mind. At dawn he rose and went to Libby's room where she slept, redolent of beer.

He sat on the edge of her bed and watched her until she woke.

"Do you know that I love you?" he said, and before she could respond: "That means I care what becomes of you. You owe me nothing. But you owe yourself a decent life."

She smiled wanly.

"I'm going to tell you something. And I don't want this repeated to your mother. You are a poor liar. You lie out of desperation and without proper planning. You lie when you don't need to. A lie is only to be used when there is no alternative. You'll get a lot more respect if you tell the truth, even when it goes against you, than if you try to cover up and get caught. If you must tell a lie, make it as close to the truth as possible. You should plan your lies. Save them for those terrible times when you have no other choice. And don't ever quote me, because I'll deny I said it."

Libby pulled herself up in the bed, hugged Henry hard, and fell back down asleep almost before her head hit the pillow.

For whatever reason, her lying stopped — or she became more adept.

A measure of tranquility returned to the household just as it had after the spankings when she was small. In her campaign to

win back her car she took over the household chores so ag-
gressively that she began to give orders to Margo—the first hint
of her brigadier-general era. She even did a little homework
without being nagged.

"What in the world did you say to her?" Margo said.

"I told her to shape up or I'd beat the hell out of her."

Yet year by year high school was almost more than Libby
could manage. Margo and Henry accepted the fact that she
wouldn't go to college. But what she lacked in the academic
arena she more than made up in the workplace with the same
staying power that had put her back on a pony after every fall.

The week she graduated from high school, still at age seventeen, she won a promotion to assistant manager at Burger King,
and while Thomas struggled to finish VMI she whipped herself
into a marathon of 70-hour weeks to keep up payments on a new
Tercel (for which Henry co-signed).

"How does Burger King make a profit when you doing all
that overtime?" Henry said.

"I'm three times as good as anyone else."

Henry raised an eyebrow.

"Four times as good. They're just a bunch of kids."

# 2. Thomas

Henry always hid his underwear when Thomas came home for
Christmas, along with his socks, his razor and deodorant. Over
the years it had developed into an art. Henry would split the

cache—half behind the poetry in the bedroom bookcase and half under the sweaters on the closet shelf, with a few decoys left in the bureau drawer, faded shorts or shrunken T-shirts Thomas wouldn't be seen dead in. Nor would Henry. Their sole function was to throw Thomas off the scent.

This was a greatly diminished extension of a long and smoky intramural war that had seen whole sets of tools strewn on the lawn undiscovered until the snow melted, borrowed and battered vehicles, unauthorized third-party charges from college phone booths (to the point that Henry had once had the service discontinued and physically removed the instruments from the house).

At the peak of his louthood—when he was fifteen—Thomas had rolled the Celica testing its acceleration on a dirt road where he'd had no business being. Henry's revenge had been to spray the damaged fender and doors in an unmatched shade of yellow, patch the black hardtop with silver plumber's tape, then drive the Celica to pick Thomas up after football practice. Thomas' audible anguish was among Henry's most treasured memories.

Everything about Thomas had been double fortissimo during those years. His voice rattled window panes. His physical presence swelled the walls. He had a way of sucking the milk from a glass as he upended it that made Henry want to wring his neck. But of course Henry would never do such a thing. His contempt had been silent, which meant it went unnoticed by Thomas and impaled Margo who suffered over subtleties.

Yet Henry had a secret compassion for a boy so testosterone-ridden that his life became a desperate competition for pumped-up muscles, for athletic prowess, for arcane knowledge of the inner workings of exotic automobiles or the December standings within the National Football Conference. Whose sensitivity about his own sexuality rendered him fragile as a champagne flute.

Although Thomas had a clear and cherished memory of his father, although he called his stepfather by his first name, he was most wholly Henry's own. He had been nine when Henry had come along. Now he was twenty two. Thomas had finally cleaned up his VMI requirements and was working a temporary job at Lexington until a pilot's slot became available.

When Henry married Margo he'd assumed somehow that after five or ten years the teenagers would grow up and leave home to follow productive lives of their own. Or at any rate that they would leave.

But the only one to stay away was Marty, while the others came back and back—Sandra and Ed with the three Muppets for mandatory holidays, Libby when she wasn't working double overtime and Thomas almost weekly until Margo had driven him out on grounds of non-productivity.

But this was Christmas with its annual armistice, ruptured only by sporadic outbursts of small-arms fire. On his first noon home when Thomas had appeared, sleepy and scratching, for breakfast wearing a deep-cut black tank top, Margo had yelled at him to go put on a shirt, brandishing the blender at him.

More upsetting than the children's presence was that of their friends in the house, not only because they tended to walk in at any hour of the day or night, but because some of them were clearly unwholesome. Libby in particular hung out with a rough-looking crew who appeared like mushrooms whenever she came home. On December 20th at two in the morning Henry walked into his own living room in his underwear to find a stunned nymph, Samantha Sweatt, staring blankly at him from his favorite reading chair. He retreated to the bedroom threatening to go back stark naked until Margo pushed him into bed and went after his cocoa.

Most disturbing of these wraith-like visitors was Bobby

Engelhardt, once a neighborhood kid, now strange and unstable in his early manhood. The boy's father, Max, had been a child-beater and wife-beater, who had played for the Chicago Bears in the 1950s, the wreck of a former athlete who still saw himself as a stud. Margo hated him for his arrogant propositions during her widowhood. Honey, Bobby's mother, was sweet but unable to stand up to Max.

Henry had only the history of all this. But Margo swore Max was subject to wild fits of rage in which he beat the boys to the point of a broken collarbone in one case, a concussion in another. "You could hear Bobby and Little Max screaming all the way across our pasture," she said. "I reported him to the police but they wouldn't do anything unless I'd sign a warrant, and I'll tell you the truth, I was afraid. The boys would come over here to get away from him."

One of Thomas' more endearing qualities was his kindness to small children or those in trouble. When Big Max raged, Thomas had hauled Little Max around on his bike like a brother of his own. Bobby and Thomas were like twins. Less than a year apart, they had gone everywhere together. As often as not a place had been set for Bobby at supper.

About a year after Henry's arrival Max Engelhardt died of a stroke. In time Honey moved back to her parents' home up in the hunt country, and contact between Thomas and Bobby was lost until they met again in high school.

Margo liked Honey's father, Curt Dunning, who was active in fox hunting. He came from an old family with a lot of lovely land, and was a generous host for a hunt breakfast. When Henry met him he was less sure. The man was a retired MP commander, a whip snapper who talked about sharpening Bobby up as though he were a pencil.

During high school Bobby would turn up for a meal or a

night a few times during the course of a year. But where Thomas inclined to muscle and pinkness of skin, Bobby grew more dark and hawk-like, hollow-eyed. "He looks skinny," Thomas told them, "but he's awesome when he goes for the ball carrier. He's like a peregrine." Thomas knew all about peregrines. Thomas applied the word "awesome" to everything from astrophysical genius to massive bowel movements, both of which he enjoyed discussing at mealtimes. His heroes were astronauts and professional football players. Henry was grateful when his growth stopped at five feet eleven and encouraged him to concentrate on math and the sciences when he failed to make the jayvees at VMI.

During Thomas' rat year in Lexington Bobby disappeared. But summer brought them together again when Bobby found Thomas a job on the construction crew where he worked.

Bobby seemed to have settled. He had a nice girl. He had an old Mustang with Cragar custom wheels. Thomas said he was making good money and looked enviously at the Cragars.

There was just a hint that Bobby wasn't always happy about his grandfather. But when Henry and Margo met Colonel Dunning at a wedding reception he waxed almost rhapsodic about their relationship. "Greatest guy in the world if he can just lick that temper. We're working on it, believe you me." It felt somehow to Henry as though the Colonel were trying to sell an old car he knew too well.

After that Bobby vanished again.

Henry didn't know Bobby had been in the Army until Bobby appeared over Christmas of Thomas' junior year (second-class year, they said at VMI). Whether he had enlisted at the Colonel's wish or against it was not clear, but Thomas was convinced that military service was an escape from home. It obviously suited Bobby—lean and trim in a uniform with Airborne wings. His girl Tanya hovered about him like a butterfly. He was driving a 280Z. He and Thomas spoke in obscure military terms or roared off in the 280Z to Georgetown where you could drink at eighteen.

Henry and Margo worried, but the holidays ended without event. Thomas returned to a less-than-successful spring semester. Bobby shipped out to Germany.

One Saturday in the spring of Thomas' final year Henry was taking a nap in the bedroom. No one was home. But there was a sound in the living room. "Henry!" called a voice. "Where the hell are ya?"

Before Henry could find his Pumas an apparition appeared at his bedroom door—Colonel Dunning in combat fatigues, with a Colt .45 in his belt. This preposterous person Henry hardly knew had walked into his house like a brother-in-law.

"Where's Bobby? Have you seen Bobby? I heard he'd been here with Tommy."

It took a minute to determine that the Tommy in question was Thomas. The rest of the message was clear if not credible: Despite the Colonel's valiant efforts Bobby had turned criminal. The range of offenses included threatening his mother with a gun, beating up his girlfriend, forging seventeen checks including a large one against his mother's account, and possibly breaking into a gas station in Columbus, Georgia. Colonel Dunning had sworn out a felony warrant for him and was ready to make a citizen's arrest on sight. Bobby was currently AWOL from Ft. Benning, said the Colonel ominously, and very likely close by at this moment. Clearly he wished to conduct a room-to-room search. He seemed unaware that he himself was a trespasser if not quite a housebreaker.

It was all so outlandish that Henry ushered him out the way you would lead a large muddy dog over a clean rug. Then he went back to his nap. He hadn't seen Bobby in four months.

The next Saturday when Thomas came home Henry described the scene to him. Thomas listened with care and promised to investigate. Sunday night he reported in before leaving for school.

"As far as I can tell, everybody's lying," he said. "Tanya says he never touched her, though they did break up last week. Bobby says none of it's true, that Colonel Dunning tried to beat him up one too many times and he knocked him down and walked out. There may really be a warrant out on him. I couldn't get a solid answer on that. He swears he's not AWOL."

"Where did you see him?" Henry said.

"In the Manassas Mall parking lot."

Henry frowned. "But where is he staying?"

"In his car, I guess. He had some air-head girl from Georgia with him."

Thomas appeared not to be upset by all this, but Henry found it disturbing and told Margo so. He'd seen the sort of kids who hung around shopping malls at night.

"Why are you telling me?" she said.

"It's just very difficult for me to understand why we have to be inflicted with beatings and forgery and thievery. This is not the way we've raised our children—"

"You're not inflicted with anything. Our children are lambs."

"How about goats," he said watching over his glasses to see if it got a piece of a smile.

Two hours after Thomas had left for VMI there was a knock at the front door. "What the hell—" said Henry heaving his body out of bed. It was 11:30. The knock recurred. The two dogs were turning themselves inside out.

It was Bobby asking for Thomas, or lacking Thomas, to use the phone. With him was a bedraggled girl with a black eye. Neither of them looked as though they'd slept for days, but they were sober as far as Henry could tell.

Bobby spent fifteen minutes trying to reach his company headquarters—or anybody that would take a message. He'd be twelve hours late. He was on his way.

The girl fell back on a kitchen chair and slept with her mouth open. She wore a flimsy cotton print dress that rode up her thighs. No stockings. Dusty sandals. Somehow the total effect was erotic. Henry tried not to look.

Fifteen minutes later they had gone. They refused food but the girl took a glass of water. No one offered to pay for the phone. Henry framed a speech about it, but Margo was asleep when he went back to the bedroom.

He had also noticed that Bobby called him Henry without the courtesy of asking.

The next time Thomas phoned home for money Margo grilled him about Bobby, with Henry at the kitchen table pretending to read the Outlook section.

"That poor child," she said when she hung up.

"What?"

"Nothing—it's just that he's always falling into traps. He's like one of those fuzzy things in the Pacman game whose main function is to get gobbled up. Only he doesn't know it. He keeps thinking he's a real person."

"What's he done now?"

Margo glared at him. "You're as bad as Curtis Dunning. Why don't you go make a citizen's arrest?"

Bobby was in the stockade at Ft. Benning. All the money he'd been saving would have to go for restitution and lawyers. He'd been forging checks to keep up with the girl Henry had seen in the kitchen.

"She didn't look like a femme fatale to me," Henry said, aware that he was lying.

"Men never recognize them. Certainly not a lamb like Bobby."

If Margo had been less indulgent perhaps Henry could have been less irritated at Bobby's erratic appearances through the spring and summer. He never knocked. He ate—in small amounts—without asking. He helped himself to the TV. Once he turned up high on something in Libby's bedroom at two in the morning. Libby pushed him gently to the front door, then turned to meet Henry's outrage.

"Really, Daddy!" she said. "You don't have to protect me."

"But—"

"I grew up with him! He's my blood brother."

"What about his beating women?"

"Sometimes he goes a little crazy, that's all. You just have to know how to handle him."

Nor would she discuss it further. Bobby continued to walk in and to call Henry Henry. Henry reserved judgment, then moved a pace closer to Bobby's camp after two particularly annoying calls from Colonel Dunning.

"Was there a message?" Margo said.

"Only that Bobby is never to set foot in his grandfather's house again. More dark suggestions that he's a fugitive from justice whom I have no business harboring. Apparently he's been discharged from the Army now—honorable, I think. I'm sure Dunning would have told me if it had been less than honorable."

"Then he's eligible for college support."

"I suppose so," said Henry. "Doesn't his mother have any say in any of this? All my contacts are with the Colonel."

"Honey? She's weaker than Bobby."

Then the issue of Bobby receded as Thomas spent the summer reverting to puberty. He'd missed graduating by three credits and was making it up at the community college in Manassas. The rest of his time he divided between a lifeguard's job and growing roots into the couch before the TV. He came in at 4:00 a.m. and slept until 2:00 the next day. He took 25-minute showers. He wore red gym shorts and muscles. He stank of Aramis. He declared a moratorium on lawn cutting, now that he was employed elsewhere. He bullied Libby and his mother. He consumed metric yards of food. Finally he so enraged Margo that she exiled him from early July to almost September when he reappeared and cut the grass. "White flag," he said. "I got homesick."

Henry renegotiated the armistice in return for a pledge to rebuild the corner fence line—for pay. But two days later Thomas again disappeared, to take the temporary recruiting post in the VMI admissions office.

"Do you realize this will be the first fall we'll have the house to ourselves?"

"I've invited Sandra to visit with the children."

So the fence work was postponed until Christmas vacation when Thomas amazed Henry by ordering the stakes and wire on his own initiative, then recruiting Bobby as helper. In the first day they had four hundred feet of stakes driven and corner posts in place.

"He wants something," Henry said. "He's never thrown me a line without a hook in it."

"I think he wants to please you, and—"

Henry eyed her over his glasses.

"And I think he wants to invite Bobby for Christmas. He has no place to go."

Henry pictured the obscene pile of gifts under the Christmas tree, the exchange mart of no less than seven adults, three small children and relatives in New Hampshire, Atlanta, and New Orleans. Would Bobby be obliged to sit watching the ritual orgy of unwrapping?

Margo's real genius was answering unasked questions. "He'd come in for dinner Christmas afternoon, then stay with us for a few more days."

Henry put on his parka and walked out to help the boys with the fence for a while. The barbed wire was awkward to unroll, stretch, staple. Thomas and Bobby were grateful for the extra pair of hands. It was a cold, clear afternoon. As they worked the sun dropped and the sky grew gold behind the minutely etched maples and pin oaks at the top of the ridge where the house sprawled like a luxury liner with its fifty yellow eyes. The talk among the three was of hammer, stretching tool, bracing of corner posts, quiet as the darkening hills, breath frosting slightly with the words' formation.

They spoke of how it had been a dozen years before, playing horseshoes together, making special rules for Little Max.

"Not so little now," said Bobby. "He's seventeen—six-three and still growing."

Henry paid them each $75.00—seven dollars an hour. Competitive for area labor.

For the holidays Bobby took up residence in Thomas' old basement burrow. It was cluttered and warm. It had a bunk. It smelled male. Thomas slept in Marty's old bedroom, made over now for guests.

There was to be a New Year's party, with much to prepare. Libby and Thomas pledged money and help if a few of their friends could be included—but it was Bobby, Margo reported, who pitched in most willingly. "Thomas just sat there while Bobby tidied up by the porch, carried in wood, vacuumed, fixed the stereo so all the speakers work again. I wish we had one like that, Henry. He really is a lamb."

Henry was loyal. "I've heard that Thomas is good with other mothers," he said.

Margo sniffed.

On New Year's Eve, before the party, Henry called Thomas and Libby for a private conference. "This is law," he said. "If any one of your friends drinks too much to drive I'm holding you personally responsible for getting them home for the night. I don't want any highway fatalities coming from this party—understand?"

They understood. Three boys from Libby's high school class had died in back-road crashes.

Henry endured parties for Margo's sake and tried not to be caustic about them afterward, though he seldom wholly succeeded. This time most of the adults were country people if not farmers—retired military, a veterinarian, a real estate broker—who had one or two horses to ride or hunt. These were Margo's friends. Everyone brought dishes or champagne to buttress the feast she had been preparing all week. On the whole Henry found the wives more interesting than the husbands, but he dutifully talked football and tended bar. Perhaps fifteen couples came, all in party clothes.

The young interested him more than any adult. Male and female, their frailty was painful to watch, with the possible exception of Libby, who was now showing signs of having been to generals' school when it came to social situations.

But the others froze into sexually segregated pods, watched to see who was watching them, drank much too fast. One effeminate boy with a defiant mustache was already stumbling at 10:30.

And there was a subdued crisis from which Henry was carefully excluded. He became aware of Libby trotting back and forth, conferring urgently with one or another of her girl friends, upstairs and down, rolling her eyes in exasperation. No, she didn't want help. No, she couldn't stop. Something about a hysterical girl downstairs. At one point Henry saw a car's lights heading down toward the barn and wondered crossly who it was. Libby shoved him away from the window. Never mind—she'd take care of it.

Eventually the car returned and he forgot it trying to put an elderly lady at ease. Someone's mother, a little lost, a little bit deaf.

Midnight came and went. Too many champagne bottles were opened. The feast was served, scarcely less obscene in its bounty than the Christmas gift exchange. Henry improved his own evening by informing the contributor of a chocolate mousse that it had a wonderful vaginal texture, then quietly watched to see how long it would take her to pass the quote to a friend. One minute and ten seconds.

By one-thirty the company departed, leaving only the hard-core drinkers gathered around the fireplace. None was over twenty-two except Margo, presiding.

Henry spent half an hour collecting plates and sloshing them clean enough for the washer. About two he gave up and fell into bed. By whatever time Margo arrived he was deeply asleep. He'd had one Scotch-and-water all night.

As usual he came wide awake at six, hugged his sleeping wife for fifteen minutes, couldn't stand the inactivity, rose and put on his sweat suit.

In the living room, the dining room, the TV room, the

kitchen, the remains of the party lay about like the wreckage of a great medieval battle. Someone had run the dishes he'd rinsed through the washer. Some of the more vulnerable casseroles and dips had been wedged into the refrigerator. Otherwise the remains of the celebration were intact. A body—Libby's boyfriend Ivan—lay wrapped in a sleeping bag by the cold fireplace. In the kitchen sink was a teddy bear with wet legs. Henry transferred it to the guest shower to drip. Then he went to work on the mess.

Fifteen minutes later a woozy-looking girl he remembered as Gretchen appeared, refused coffee or aspirin, fished a half gallon of orange juice from the refrigerator, drank four glasses in a row, groped her way back toward Libby's bedroom.

Fifteen minutes after that Libby herself emerged from the basement.

"Where's my teddy bear?"

"In the shower, drying. Why was it here?"

"Gretchen threw up on it."

"Gretchen just barely made it to the refrigerator to consume half a carton of orange juice. Four glasses—one, two, three, four. Just like that. That's a very rough paraphrase of a poem by e.e. cummings. How do you like your blue-eyed hangover now, Mister Death?"

Libby looked blank.

"Were you downstairs visiting Bobby?" he said returning the look.

Libby sighed. "I have to tell you now. We kept it quiet last night so we wouldn't mess up the party. There was a big fight— Bobby and Thomas—over Tanya. Honestly! Bobby broke up with her ten months ago, but he went crazy when he saw her down there with Thomas. I mean, like, wild. Thomas really tried not to hurt him at first, but then *he* went crazy and there was blood all over, and Bobby *still* wanted to fight and we shoved him out the door to cool off before Thomas bashed his whole head in.

"But then he didn't come back. All he had on was a light sweater. I thought I saw him heading out for the road, but we drove out and couldn't find him and then Ivan went back by the barn looking. That's what you saw. . . ."

"Where is he now?"

"We never found him."

"Could he have gone back to his apartment?"

Libby stared at him. "You didn't understand? He didn't have any other place. He spent Christmas Eve at Rose's Motel."

"Good Lord! How badly was he hurt? How much had he had to drink? We should go look now—" He glanced out the window. It was just coming light.

Libby was, in fact, on her way to wake Ivan to continue the search. But neither of them seemed to feel any life-or-death urgency. Despite the bleeding Bobby had still had a lot of fight in him when they'd pushed him out. Libby insisted he hadn't been drunk—just crazy. Ivan pointed out that paratroopers knew how to survive in enemy territory.

The phrase rang unpleasantly in Henry's head as Libby and Ivan went out to feed the horses and check the barn for Bobby again. He went to wake Margo, then together they exhumed Thomas, who emerged frowsy, with one black eye. "I couldn't make him quit," he kept insisting. "I tried to wrestle him down but he still kept at me. He tried to shove his knee into my face. So I finally had to hit him."

"With that?" Henry pointed to the VMI class ring, notorious as the heaviest anywhere—sort of a formal-wear blackjack.

"I had it on at the time." Thomas was embarrassed, but he was still angry at Bobby. "He can't go home because he went crazy there. He can't even go back to Rose's. The last night he stayed there he broke in."

"You mean for Christmas Eve?" Margo said.

"Merry Christmas, huh? But it's his own fault. He keeps making it worse for himself."

Libby and Ivan returned from the barn to report that the tack room door was open, but no Bobby anywhere—not in any of the stalls, not in the hayloft, not the toolroom. Margo insisted that Thomas go check at Rose's but they hadn't seen him either.

In the end they gave it up. Henry and Margo and the girls tackled the house, which took all morning. Thomas and Ivan went to finish the lower paddock fence line. When a forecast called for six inches of snow before midnight, Henry went out, hooked up the tractor blade, got gas at the pump by the barn, dug an extra pin for the three-point hitch out of the toolroom. By the time he returned to the house a steady fine snow was rattling the leaves along the woods' edge. First snow. Tomorrow's commute would be awful, but on this dark afternoon the peace was private and complete.

Henry went in to read by the fire, out of the television's reach. As dark approached he heard the kitchen door slam. The boys in from fencing. Then the sound of Margo's call—trouble and fear transmitted in the single word: "Henry!"

It brought him to his feet.

"They've found Bobby. Wrapped in horse blankets, up in that empty loft over the tack room. He's not moving."

Ivan was trying to steady his hands as he leafed through the phone book. "Thomas is still out there," he said.

Henry made the call. Yes, an emergency, possibly a dead man. Rescue squad and patrol car needed. Ivan was meanwhile explaining they'd seen the light in the toolroom and gone looking again and found him almost by chance. The light Henry had left on.

Somehow the dispatcher was unfamiliar with their area and took a great deal of time getting directions. He asked Henry to drive out to Route 29 to meet the ambulance. Heavy snow now, he said.

Always it seemed when death was close Henry found it hard to get enough air into his lungs. He grabbed his jacket, shoved his mud boots on and hurried out the door.

Before he could scrape the windows of the Suburban he saw headlights and a flashing beacon coming in the long driveway, almost lost in the blowing snow at first, materializing then as a sheriff's patrol car. It was as close to a blizzard as Henry had seen in years. More like home.

Margo appeared in the murk, zipping up her jacket, went to the patrol car, opened the door, then climbed in. Henry watched them continue down slowly toward the barn. He went back to the Suburban, started it. The windows were opaque again. He turned on the wipers and crept out toward the highway. The hospital was ten miles away. In this mess, there'd be time to wait.

Eighteen hours. A light sweater. Henry wasn't sure a body could survive it, even out of the wind. Even wrapped in blankets. Temperature in the low twenties last night. Barely above freezing all today. Now the snow. Except that Henry had left the tool-room light on, they'd never have found him. Not for days.

With no weight in the back the Suburban wanted to slip on the grade. Henry lightened his foot and coaxed it to the top. "If I'd been Bobby," he said to the windshield wipers, "I'd have hit him with the maul. Serve him right if they charge him with manslaughter. That'd take care of his Air Force slot." He sighed. "Then we'd have him home forever."

He clapped his mouth shut, appalled at his own venom.

"Listen to your priorities, will you," he thought, "with poor Bobby probably dead in the loft."

But Bobby was not dead. By the time Henry had led the ambulance to the barn the sheriff's deputies had determined not only that he was alive but that he was wanted on a felony warrant for forgery.

Margo drew Henry aside and put her arms around his neck. "For the longest time," she said quietly, "we couldn't tell. The sheriff's man went up there. Then he didn't say anything. Just worked over him with a flashlight. And he still didn't say anything. Finally he said, 'I'm getting a pulse.' Then, 'It's very weak.' Then, 'He's breathing.' He tried to get Bobby to answer but he couldn't. Then he radioed them to hurry with the ambulance."

Henry, Margo, and the young people huddled in the barn aisle watching as the Rescue Squad scrambled up into the cramped space over the tack room, got a faint response from Bobby, checked him for hand and foot movement. They strapped him to a board stretcher and lowered him to the ground. Outside snow swirled in the headlights.

Then it was over. Ambulance gone. Patrol cars gone. Darkness and driving snow. Silence. The group trudged to the house, eventually followed to the hospital and waited by the emergency room for reports.

Hypothermia but no frostbite. Possibility of broken ribs, skull fracture. He was conscious now.

"How hard did you hit him?" said Margo. And there followed a lengthy subdued wrangle in the hallway as Thomas justified himself over and over: Bobby wouldn't quit. . . . He tried to knee me. . . . He was crazy. . . . He hadn't seen Tanya for almost a year.

Little Max arrived — six-three, more massive than his father, but easy. He let Thomas off the hook, agreeing that Bobby did go crazy sometimes.

But only Little Max was allowed to see Bobby, while Thomas was made to wait outside. A sheriff's deputy stood guard. The patient's next stop would be jail.

Home at last, Henry drove the young from the TV room with Strauss—Herbert von Karajan wryly conducting the Vienna Philharmonic in the New Year's celebration. Waltzes, polkas, a gallop—an hour and a half of old Austria's glory. Stereo simulcast. Dazzling color and light and sound. Lippizaner stallions. Kathleen Battle in a scarlet gown—American, black, gorgeous against the backdrop of the all-male orchestra, singing "Voices of Spring." Flawless couples waltzing the aisles of Schoenbrunn Palace.

Finally, in the great hall of the Musikverein the audience was clapping with the Radetzky March, the traditional closing of the New Year's concert. Conductor von Karajan smiled and waved them into silence after the first refrain, then brought them back at the repeat. Wide shots of packed orchestra, balconies, tight shots of small groups, luminous faces, upholstered gentlemen, shapely ladies in gowns all the colors of the rainbow.

Henry glared at the television set as though it were leaking blood onto the floor.

# 12

———— •◆• ————

The doctor had insisted he lose more weight. So Henry was experimenting with a diet where you drank three quarts of water—morning, noon, and night—each within the space of half an hour.

The idea of the diet was that all this water flushed the salt out of your system, in turn releasing water from the tissues—that it gave absolution to your liver, which in turn released the cells from storing fat, and that it filled you up and killed your appetite.

The system made you go to the bathroom a lot, which was difficult with Henry's forty-mile commute to Washington. He was running a test on Saturday morning (he thought of it as a dry run) to see whether he could finish going to the bathroom by eight if he had consumed his morning quart by six-fifteen.

"What are you doing up at this hour?" Libby appeared in a knee-length T-shirt that said LAUDERDALE! She was now an elderly twenty—a newly hired airline employee endowed with good travel and health benefits and boyfriends who called after eleven at night.

"I always wake up early once February's done."

"When are you going to open the birthday present from your brother?" She glanced at a book-shaped object in brown paper behind the salt and pepper and the paper napkins on the kitchen table. The package had sat for a week untouched, addressed to Henry in Joey's erratic hand.

"Why don't you call him Uncle Joey?"

Libby grinned. The question was the answer. Joey was nobody's idea of an uncle.

Poor Joey wasn't anything, exactly. Well, he was a charismatic clergyman in a sect so obscure Henry could never remember its name. Before that he'd sold advertising for the Nashua *Telegraph.* Perhaps he still did. Before that he'd been a state trooper. Before that he'd been a fund-raiser for the Boston Symphony. A long time before that he'd abandoned four or five college careers. He was ten years younger than Henry, which would make him fifty-two now. It was impossible to picture Joey in his fifties.

The birthday present was a move in a game of guilt they had inherited from their mother. Last fall on Joey's birthday Henry had made the mandatory annual phone call and the annual promise of a gift, followed by his annual failure to follow through.

There were so many things Henry and Joey couldn't discuss that telephone calls were difficult after the first eight bars.

They could not, for instance, discuss Henry's three marriages. Nor his stepchildren nor his adopted Libby. Nor the family heirlooms that had become the property of previous wives. Nor Joey's only child, Naomi, product of his very loins, student at Oral Roberts, rightful inheritor of all remaining Calef family possessions, including the Aaron Willard banjo clock that hung in Henry's living room.

They could not discuss God.

They could not discuss Joey's young manhood. Sooner or later they would have to discuss Mother's ashes.

Henry sighed, thinking of the baby brother syndrome—all the world's petted Teddys and Billys and Joeys who could never outgrow their diminutives, last sons in high-achiever families whose successes were in direct proportion to their failures, in the degree to which they could outrage righteous siblings, be they presidents of the senior class, the Seacoast Steel Corporation, or the United States of America.

Joey had fit this mold—a breaker of family taboos and his own bones. A bright child, homely, cheerful, lazy in the sense that he would expend great energy to avoid work. "Undisciplined" was an inadequate word for Joey. He was an insurgent battling social order in any form.

The first time he broke his wrist was in a failed attempt to leap from the roof of the A&P to Skillings' Hardware when pursued by the A&P produce manager after he and Marston Arbuckle had engaged in back-alley warfare with rotten potatoes. Joey was eight at the time.

A year later he was hospitalized after ingesting a combination of Coca-Cola and Dutch cleanser because Anthony Crutchfield had told him it would make him drunk.

At ten he and Marston Arbuckle were arrested for breaking into a tennis racket factory, then trying to escape in the cruiser of the policemen who were investigating the broken window they'd climbed through.

These were the headliners. More typical was the fact that Joey was never where he should have been, late to everything, unprepared for all events, undisturbed by all blandishments. Not simply undisturbed—delighted. Inverse achievement.

He was pushed from grade to grade, learning more than he'd admit. No teacher could bear to have him a second time.

His last arrest was at fourteen for borrowing Marston Arbuckle's grandfather's 1938 Packard without asking, running it
without oil until the pistons froze in their cylinders, and aban-
doning it in despair on the Worcester Turnpike. They were jailed
overnight by the state police before their fathers came.

Joey hated jail. He took pains after that to avoid the criminal
justice system. In high school his achievements ranged from
brilliant (dramatics) to marginal (Latin, French, history, al-
gebra, geometry, government, English, biology, chemistry,
gym, shop).

In the fall of Joey's first senior year in high school, their father
died. Henry was twenty-seven, teaching history at Colby, married to Ruth the math teacher. The force of their mother's
collapse fell less on him than on Joey, who was her keeper and
prisoner at home. Henry had hardly been in Boston—between
the Army and college—for a decade and had grown away from
both parents.

His father had been a moderately successful broker on State
Street whom Henry had loved from a distance, sharing with him
an amused, unspoken conspiracy to contain Mother's histrionics.
How important the game had been became apparent only in its
loss. Not that his death wouldn't have been enough to send even a
stable wife into a tailspin—from apparently vigorous health to
twisted cadaver on the kitchen floor in the space of fifteen
minutes.

Henry and Ruth stayed around until the weekend after the
funeral, then returned to Waterville in the belief that Joey and
Mother were settled if not comfortable. Only when Joey turned
up on their porch the following April with four F's and a D did
Henry begin to get the picture. Joey was weighing a hitch with
the Marines against suicide on the railroad tracks.

The trip home to prop Mother up and bail Joey out was the

first of a long series, as Henry took up the roles of surrogate father and advocate. Joey was trundled through a succession of private schools, with multiple repeats of his failed courses until his college-requirement grades emerged like reluctant tomato plants through the flinty soil of his study habits.

There followed single-semester appearances at Northeastern, Tufts, and Emerson, all within commuting distance of Mother, all ending in dropped courses and incompletes.

Finally Henry persuaded Colby to take him on, and for five months he lived with them in Waterville enduring Ruth's compulsive sniping but getting B's and one A. They all spent Christmas at home exulting in his success. In February Mother summoned him in the dead of night.

"I've got to go back," said Joey, his face — his whole body — in torment.

"Stay. She'll survive," said Henry.

"I can't."

"You'll be an old man in two years," said Ruth. "Look at you."

But he went. He got a job at the Waltham Watch plant, then tried summer stock in Ogunquit. The twice-weekly commute home was too much.

At twenty-four he took up with the enemy. He fell in love with another woman.

Joey hadn't done well with girls. He stood five feet eight to Henry's six-one, although he was stocky. He could beat Henry at any physical competition. But he'd had acne and a silly cowlick that caused a bad self-image — which caused bad posture. His high school and college years were strewn with the wreckage of his hopeless loves locked in a secret chamber of his brain.

The girl was all wrong for him, Mother told Henry on the phone. She was a beautician, she was Italian and Catholic. Joey was college material. Joey was seriously considering the Moody Bible Institute.

"In Chicago?" said Henry, reflecting that the girl sounded perfect for Joey. "I thought you needed to have him at home."

"If Chicago is necessary I will make the sacrifice."

There followed a clearly implied suggestion that Henry—now divorced and working for the government in Washington—could come back to Newton. "You wouldn't have to live in the same house with me," she said.

Mother was a genteel country minister's daughter who was becoming a painter of great promise when she'd married Dad in 1920. She had continued to paint summers when Henry was little, then gave it up to volunteer for church work during Joey's boyhood. She belonged to a mild Congregationalist parish, her faith growing in inverse proportion to Dad's apostasy, then to Henry's.

She was a large, immensely powerful woman who enslaved her sons by being weak. When Henry brought a can of beer home she contracted influenza and ran high fevers until he agreed to stop drinking. But then he left home. When she tried to get him 4-F status for asthma he signed up for the Army. He hadn't had asthma since he was six.

But Joey couldn't escape until too late. He and Mother were entombed with the relics of Dad's life. She got dizzy spells, so he had to drive her to shop and to church. She developed eczema, so he had to cook and do the dishes.

Although Dad had provided comfortably for her she hoarded her money and asked for help, so Joey had to chip in his mite from his hundred and one part-time jobs. Henry sent money, too. Henry was good at sending money.

The third Christmas after Dad's death Henry gave Mother a

set of oils, brushes, and six canvases. She cried of course. He was sweet but it was too late.

Then miraculously she began to paint again. She made Joey sit for a portrait and showed it to her hairdresser, who commissioned an oil to be done from an ancient, blurry snapshot of an elderly couple with a 1927 Whippet in the background. Henry thought she rendered the Whippet better than the grandparents, but the hairdresser's memory was as fuzzy as the photo. She loved the oil enough for a permanent and six weeks of shampoos and sets.

More significantly she hung the painting in the shop, and Mother was suddenly in the portrait business. The first ten were all dead people, but then came a bride, then a child. Mother was great with children. She told them stories and had tea parties with them while she sketched. A few students began coming to the house.

What she couldn't stand was to be alone nights. She couldn't sleep. She was afraid that men would get in through the cellar door. So Joey had to stay home.

And finally he fell in love with Heather Tomasino despite Mother's efforts. When she forbade him to bring that girl into the house, he led Heather up to his bedroom and shut the door.

Mother took to her bed, coughing and sweating. Joey took Heather to see *The High and the Mighty.*

Mother locked her bedroom door and refused to speak. Joey told the door he was getting married and moving out. Mother swallowed barbiturates until she vomited and collapsed by the toilet.

Joey had her pumped out, gave Heather up, and came home. But his mother love was blown forever. He went through the paces because he couldn't fight her but his heart was a dead cigar.

When he finally escaped at age thirty-one it was by marrying Harriet Thrush, the daughter of the Congregationalist minister, and committing himself to matriculation at the Gideon Seminary in the Fenway near the New England Conservatory of Music and the Boston Museum of Fine Arts, which pleased Mother greatly. It was as though he could absorb culture by proximity while he was studying for the ministry. He and Harriet would live at Gideon's married couples' quarters, not more than ten miles from Newton.

He stuck it out for three semesters, running back and forth to Mother. Naomi was born. Money ran out. In 1968 they moved to Plymouth, New Hampshire, where Joey got a truck driver's job. He gave Henry his address to be used only in the event of Mother's stroke, heart attack, or major surgery.

She did her best. She called Henry nightly in hysterics for three weeks. Then she settled down to become a professional grande dame, six years older than the century, full of energy, wrinkles, and amusing anecdotes, surrounded by devoted clients and students.

Henry and Joey resumed their Christmas visits and found her more bearable but discovered they disliked one another's wives (Henry was on his second) and were uncomfortable with each other. Joey and Harriet had a way of talking about love that Henry found particularly nauseating—a fixation upon the agape that put them somehow in a superloving status, floating happily above the masses of unwashed. Like Henry. Worst, he realized that Joey was feeling sorry for him, and he thought, *My God, this man is turning into his own mother.*

But false, false . . . wrong in any rational world, for Joey must hate this great lady who had cut his young manhood into patches and sewn them into a quilt. Henry confronted him.

"We've forgiven her," Joey said beatifically in the kitchen.

"Her beauty outshines the pain she has left behind. Only after the storm of repentance do we pass to the still waters. . . ."

Even worse because Henry's Edith grew spastic in the presence of God. She was an emotional cripple whom he'd rescued because she had no place to go and because he loved her young body. Marrying her had been the mistake you made in the sixties when you wanted to hold a respectable job and live with a girl. A marriage to disaster, to depression, to social and physical denial. When the marriage collapsed Henry swore there'd never be another. Then he met Margo.

His mother waited a modest interval after the wedding to be sure he wasn't going to get divorced again. Then she called to say she had a few family things she thought he ought to have. This was the opening move in a ritual Henry had played in twice before, and he didn't want a third game. It was a no-win situation that placed him at midpoint between his mother's contradictory dicta—to value human love to the exclusion of all else, and to love family possessions as his link to his noble forebears in New England and, very long ago, in old England.

In his two previous marriages she had passed down to him for eternal safekeeping two Shaker ladder-back chairs (Ruth) and a set of British pewterware (Edith). Both bequests were given on condition that they never leave the family.

He had abandoned all possessions when he left Ruth; Edith had grabbed the pewterware when she left him. On both occasions Mother made it clear she was beside herself with disappointment and disapproval. She wanted the damn things back. She wanted Henry to get them back—if necessary by breaking and entering in the night. She threatened to go after them herself.

Henry knew better than to remind her that these were material things and thus of no more than earthly value, but she knew what he was thinking and answered him anyhow. She said they were family possessions that had taken on human associations from the great forebears connected with them.

Henry could not resist pointing out that the pewter set was one she had acquired herself on a 1948 trip to New Brunswick. She denied it in the face of facts they both knew.

These conversations frequently took place between one and two in the morning when she would call because she was physically sick at the loss of the Calef family heritage and because she had the mistaken idea that there were special phone rates between midnight and four in the morning. She made the calls about marriage number one during marriage number two. She made the calls about marriages one and two after marriage number three. "It does give me a certain sense of continuity," Henry noted to Margo. Margo forbore.

When Henry finally hung up on his mother forever and unplugged the phone in the night, she began calling Margo—not, of course, to pursue the matter of old lost treasures but to offer new old treasures. She wept that she had alienated her eldest son. She said she had a truckload of things he must come for before she was forced by infirmity to give up her home. She said these were things Libby should have, which came closer to the target. To date Libby had been clearly if silently classified as a non-descendant.

When all else failed she threatened to die. It wasn't quite so absurd any more.

Three years after Henry and Margo were married, his mother had fallen and smashed her hip, and after the flurry of emergency flights and hospital visits by sons, wives, ministers, parishioners, and neighbors, a coalition was formed to help her keep her house and independence—with the assistance of Meals on Wheels and an endlessly energetic church secretary named Lila whom Henry had dated in high school. Two facts emerged during her time of crisis: that her days of independence were numbered—and that she would never tolerate an institution. She'd behaved atrociously in the convalescent home, refusing to eat, accusing them of grand larceny and attempted murder by poison. "If they *hadn't* sedated her," Lila told Henry, "she'd have had the FBI in there. As it was, she wrote to Robert Schuller and Billy Graham."

Finally the third offer of "things Libby ought to have" weakened Henry's resolve. After a night of dark misgivings, he cleaned the hay and spare parts out of the Suburban and headed north on I-95 with Margo, "on condition that she understands I don't want a damn thing from her," he said.

Margo was impatient. "Why do you have to be so suspicious about it? She irritates me, too, you know, but I don't talk about her as though she's the enemy. You seem to forget that she's just a fragile little old lady."

"Why does a nail distrust a hammer? She's my mother. I've known her all my life."

But he was shaken by the change in her. She'd lost forty pounds in the course of the year. When she got out of bed at all, she moved with a walker. The bed itself was a squirrel's nest of food caches, Kleenex, magazines, books, a Bible, notes, all hidden under the sheets and beneath the pillows. The squalor of the bedridden. The smell of stale talcum permeated everything.

Despite himself Henry had to fight back his suspicions. He'd seen her perform her sweet-courage-in-the-teeth-of-pain role before.

*I have become a monster,* he told himself as she led them slowly to see the big surprise she'd been saving for them. *The woman is eighty-four years old. She has a metal hip. And all I can think of is, she's going to twist my head again.*

The surprise was in the guest room—Joey's old room—

converted into an upstairs studio for her painting. Mother moved the walker perhaps three inches at a bite, with Margo and Henry obliged to follow and wait with her, for she was speaking as she walked—in a barely audible voice. How much she had looked forward to their coming. How much closer she had become to God. How Dr. Schuller had personally answered her letters. Twice. The nights were almost bearable now. How her painting had taken on new strength, as though God were using her to hold His brush. She explained in a sort of gay little joke to Margo that Henry was her last failure, that she wished she knew how to manipulate her sons so she could move Henry to hear Jesus' knock at the door.

As they approached the easel Henry saw over her shoulder a very large canvas, nearly finished, of the boy Christ preaching to an attentive group of elders. The setting was contemporary: the men in three-piece suits, Christ in shorts and a sweater, his curly hair glistening with gold highlights, the most subtle of halos. The model for the child was a photograph of Henry at age twelve, held to the easel by a thumbtack.

"My gift to the church," Mother breathed.

"Wonderful!" said Margo.

"Gotcha!" said Henry softly, turning away.

After twenty-four hours of talk and tea Henry pointed out that they had brought the Suburban.

The what?

"A truck," he said. "You asked us to bring a truck."

"What for?" said his mother.

Henry drew a deep breath. After all these years this fragile little old lady could still thrust him into a helpless rage. "Furniture," he said carefully. "Things for Libby."

"How old is Libby now?" said his mother looking vague.

Eventually she sent him to the basement, where he went with

a sinking heart, remembering the collection of broken and moldy discards, much of it from thirty years ago. Nothing was changed. He climbed the stairs to his mother's bedroom.

"Mother," he said. "There is nothing in the basement worthy of a trip to the dump."

"The mission table," she snapped with perfect recall. "The sofa."

"No, Mother. I did not drive five hundred miles to take home a wicker couch and the table you used for the battery radio."

"An Atwater-Kent," she said. "I was saving it for you but the furnace man stole it."

"I'm going, Mother. Goodbye." He turned and walked down the stairs again, leaving Margo to do the amenities.

"Wait!" Her voice followed him down that very stairwell as it had done and done so many times in their lifetime series of confrontations.

Five minutes later Margo came out to the Suburban where he was checking the oil. "She wants you to take the pineapple four-poster and the bureau that matches it. The mahogany one. She says you'll know."

"I know," said Henry.

"And the Aaron Willard clock."

"I don't believe it," said Henry.

"She said it's the most precious thing in the house."

"It is. Probably ten thousand by now. More, maybe. Museum piece."

"She said it was your great-grandfather's."

"And it must never leave the family. I don't want it."

"It's for Libby, Henry."

"She's twisting us again."

"She's very old now, dear. You don't have to fight her anymore."

So the clock was taken, carefully stuffed with tissue paper and cradled in blankets along with the pineapple four-poster and bureau and a cedar hope chest Mother added at the last minute. She stood with the walker at the bedroom window and watched them load. Waved them goodbye. A room in her home was stripped.

"Be sure to eat enough," called Margo.

"Drive carefully," called Mother. "Promise you'll cut back on salt."

Henry drove down the hill from the house where he had grown to manhood, filled with ritual self-hatred. He would have punished himself by driving straight through to Virginia, but Margo persuaded him to stop at the New Haven Holiday Inn.

At eleven o'clock on the night of their return home the phone rang. Margo took it, talking softly, then covered the mouthpiece.

"She wants you to bring the clock back. She says we misunderstood. She didn't mean we were to take it yet. She's very upset."

"Let her talk to Libby. It's Libby's clock now." Henry was under the covers, feigning sleep.

"You have to speak to her. She's your mother."

So Henry took the phone and grunted into it for fifteen minutes, and what it finally came to was that Joey's Harriet had understood the clock was promised to their daughter, cousin Naomi.

"Mother," said Henry, "you have given that damned clock to Libby. She believes you care about her. I never want another thing from you, but I will not return the clock."

He hung up the phone and unplugged it from its jack. He wished in his heart he could throw it out the window and never speak into it again. Knowing that Margo would once more be the object of the counterattack and subsequent siege, he instructed her to ignore it to the extent possible and under no circumstances to inform him about the size or strategy of enemy forces. "Just hold the walls," he said. "We've got enough food to survive the winter."

Even so he underestimated the opposition. After two weeks of muffled communication Harriet herself called Libby. Libby came to Henry in tears. "She says you stole it and I can't have it because it belongs to Naomi. I don't even care about the old clock. It doesn't even run!"

Henry rose up in his wrath. "Never!" he shouted. "They can take me to court! They can storm the house! I'll mount machine guns!" He lifted Libby from the floor and crushed her in his arms, alarming her even more than Harriet had done. She had heard Henry yell perhaps twice in her life. Never before had he snatched her from her feet except to spank her when she was little.

When he calmed down Henry announced that the subject of the clock was closed forever and that he would hang up if anyone so much as asked him the time of day. So for a year there was total silence, which was to say calls on special days and once a month between times. Mother spent Christmas with Joey, Harriet, and Naomi.

Joey had moved to Salem, New Hampshire, during this period and was hauling horses that ran at Rockingham racetrack. The agreement was that he would drive the forty miles to look in on Mother at least weekly. Henry was to make his usual contribution — money.

The following May, Lila called: "You've got to do something about your mother. She's not eating enough. She hasn't been downstairs since last time you were here. She's dirty, Henry. The house is a mess. I've tried calling Joey, but he doesn't want to talk to me."

She told him Joey almost never stopped by. A public health nurse came in on Thursdays, but only Lila was filling the gap, visiting daily to carry up her meals and check on her. Now Lila had been offered a new job that might take her elsewhere.

"How long since Joey's been there?"

"I'm not sure. Six weeks, maybe."

"Could you look into visiting nurses for me?"

Lila hesitated for a minute. "Yes," she said finally. "I'll try. But you should come up yourself and talk to them. They charge all outdoors, and some of them are tyrants."

Henry promised to come, then as an afterthought said, "What about you? Do you have to take that new job? I'd be willing to pay *you* all outdoors. I'd even promise to fly up to sleep with you at least once a month."

"Now, you stop that." Henry had been making these propositions since junior high school.

The next week she met him at the shuttle with lists of nursing services and prices. "She's slipping, Henry. Both her hearing and her sight are going. Some days she sleeps twenty hours."

In her bedroom after the tremulous bear hug the first thing his mother said was, "Do you have a car?"

"Why?" said Henry cautiously.

"I haven't been to church for so long. My old taxi driver died, you know. I thought perhaps you might take me. You wouldn't have to go in. You could sit in your car and read." She had been trying to get him into a church for thirty years.

Yet tonight he was seeing a stranger, a face fallen in on itself. Henry realized that in her extreme age she looked like her own father had looked in his last days—high dome, sparse white hair, sharp beak, sucked-down mouth. A dying hawk.

But she was not dead. She was still trying to con him. Taking reassurance, he sat beside her and stroked her forehead, chatting, paying attention to her. Did her TV work? Could she see it well enough? How about her radio? Could she still read a little with her glasses? What did she need other than to get him and God together?

"Joey," she said.

"How long since he's been here?"

"Can't remember. Long time."

Joey denied it. Two weeks at most. That damned Lila was a busybody. No, he would not be able to help pay for day nurses — not with Naomi in college. Why didn't Henry just leave it to him to straighten out?

All this in a phone call.

"I can't walk out of here until I know she's taken care of. If need be, I'll hire the nurses myself."

"No, don't do that."

"What, then, Joey?"

There was a long pause. "I'll send Naomi," he said finally.

Henry wasn't comfortable with it. Naomi couldn't be enslaved for very long. Joey said the Lord would help them find a solution. Henry rolled his eyes as they hung up.

Naomi would be a stopgap until the Oral Roberts fall session if necessary. But it would be hard on a young girl, to spend a summer vacation cooped up with an ancient grandmother. What bothered Henry most was that Joey would lie about visiting Mother. It never occurred to him to doubt Lila's word, perhaps because she was less inclined to drag God in.

At home Henry and Margo struggled with it. He would not ask her to take on his mother. Perhaps they could find a home nearby, he suggested, knowing it was unrealistic. The expense would be unthinkable. And she would fight them to her death.

"They'd have to double-sedate her," Margo said. "She'd be a vegetable."

"Awful," Henry said. "Remind me to die before I get like that."

In June Joey offered the solution. They would sell her house and use the money to finish the apartment over his garage. What was left over could help pay for her upkeep and nursing if the insurance fell short.

"What do you want out of the house?" Joey said.

"Not one damn thing. If you're willing to keep her with you, you can have it all."

"What about Libby?"

"Libby has the clock. That's enough."

There was a long silence. Henry could picture Harriet gesticulating wildly in the background. If so, she lost. Joey let it go.

Subsequent calls and letters reported the bare details of progress—drywall, plumbing, lights, all costly. A buyer for the house in Newton at a disappointing price.

"He's still got to poor-mouth me," Henry complained. "I told him to keep it all, and he's still got to make it sound small."

In August she was moved, not happily, but not having tantrums. She would have a nice Christian girl with her except at night.

"Wonderful!" said Henry. "Let me know if you need me to pitch in."

"Just come see her," Joey said. "We'll give her all the love we can, but you're her firstborn."

"You make me want to vomit!" Henry said, but not until he'd hung up.

Mother got her own phone and tried to call, but not often. It was hard for her to hear, hard for Henry to understand the faded voice. For the first time in his life he began to call her every week to keep her company if only with the sound of his voice.

"How are Joey and Harriet?" he asked her once.

"I don't know."

"Don't you talk to them?"

"No."

"Never?"

"Maybe once or twice."

"Once since you've been there, Mother? My God, that's been four months."

"Yes. Naomi came over a few times, but now she's gone. . . . I have nice Christian girls."

A week later Henry and Margo flew up to Boston bearing Christmas presents. A new nightie for Mother. Pictures of Libby. Sweaters for the others. Odd years were sweaters—even years, shirts.

They rented a car, drove to a motel in New Hampshire. Joey's space was limited and Harriet was teaching kindergarten thirty miles away. Joey met them and took them to a restaurant.

"Don't be shocked when you see her," he said. "She's very courageous, but there's not much strength left."

"How often do you visit her?"

"Not as much as we'd like. We've both been working so hard. I have a little church, you know."

"How often, Joey?"

"Oh, maybe every other day. Maybe twice a week some- times. She's so excited about your coming that I'm worried for her. She talks about you all the time. Poor dear, we're all she has. She's very close to the Lord now, Henry, so try not to upset her about that. . . . You two get some rest tonight, and we'll have her ready for you in the morning. She wants to be dressed and sitting in her chair."

In the hotel room Henry fumed to Margo. "He's so dishonest! He resents her more than I do. Why doesn't he just admit it instead of all this God and maple syrup?"

"Do you think he's really left her alone all this time?"

"I don't know. Probably. But why doesn't he just say she drives him crazy?"

"You should confront him if it upsets you so. You grind and grind, but you don't say a word."

Henry removed his shoes and aligned them under the bed. He pulled off his socks, tied them in a knot to show they'd been used, and put them into his suitcase. He took his glasses off, held them to the light, blew at the lenses. He climbed into bed.

"What good would it do?" he said.

The visit with Mother was a disaster. There she was in her Sunday dress, propped up in her old wing chair in a strange new room still smelling faintly of paint and mastic, crammed with her familiar dark and massive furniture — in her chair like a blind old dog waiting for dinner, unable to see it or smell it when it walked in and sat down and said *Eat me!* Joey was there waiting but no Harriet or Naomi, perhaps angry forever over a lost clock, but Joey there standing guard with his preacher's wary cordiality beside the sweet Christian girl who turned out to be a gorgon of no less than sixty, smiling as though her life depended on it.

"Now I have both my sons," Mother said holding each by the hand so that they were obliged to lean awkwardly toward her around the wing chair. She had accepted Margo's embrace as that of a stranger.

But reciprocal conversation was out of the question. She

could not hear Henry; he couldn't understand what she said and
had to ask her over and over.

"What?"

"Mike new blouse."

"I can't understand you, Mother."

She said it again, still garbled. Henry looked around for
help.

"She wants to know how you like her new house," said the
Christian girl.

"Oh! It's great! Lots of light!"

Mother didn't like it much. It wasn't home, it wasn't hers,
and it certainly wasn't private. But she was fond of her helper.
They had devotions together every day.

"We brought you a Christmas present," Henry said, but his
mother's eyes were glazed. To his horror the corners of her mouth
drew down and she began to tremble violently. She was having a
convulsion. Henry looked around for Joey, but he was gone.

Amazingly Henry and the helper became a rescue team,
lifting his mother's rigid body, carrying her to the bed as
smoothly as ballet dancers, while Margo laid back the blanket
and sheet to receive her. The helper pulled at Mother's skirt,
which had ridden up over her buttocks as she lay quaking.

"Teeth!" said Margo. The helper whirled, groped with
Mother's mouth.

Then Joey was back, too, the three hovering over the bed
while Henry froze watching them, expecting his mother to die
before his eyes.

But she lived on for two years, more and more remote from
human contact. Phone calls were hopeless. Henry sent chatty

letters with his checks, but her responses were mostly illegible when they came at all. Apparently she had been having a series of small strokes, Joey told him during one of their annual birthday conversations. Henry didn't offer to visit, nor was he invited, but birthday presents came each April from Joey, inscribed with love.

When Mother died Henry was in London chairing a panel at the Second International Conference on Family Violence. Joey urged him not to rush home—the funeral would be private. They'd have a memorial service in Newton as soon as Henry was back.

He lay in his hotel room the night he'd heard the news, trying to analyze his feelings. It was nothing like the numbing shock after his father's collapse. Rather it was as though she were not really gone and could not be gone, or perhaps it was that she had already been gone the past two years or however long it had been since she couldn't joust with him any more, or perhaps since he had watched her helpless in her spasm and had felt compassion for her in a way he had never experienced before, a pity unalloyed with human complexities, a pity you would feel for an animal, a horse down with colic perhaps.

Yet she was the human being whose orbit had most closely coincided with his for all the days of his years, whose destructive traits he'd had to struggle hardest to eradicate from his own behavior, whose whole frame of life had shaped his—his love and knowledge of painting, sculpture, music, the classics. Oddly he remembered swimming with her at Little Sebago the summer before ninth grade, she doing the breaststroke, drilling him in the first declension noun *femina* with the rhythm of her arms as they opened the water before her.

·   ·   ·

Henry agreed to the scheduling of the memorial service immediately after his trip, so that his jet lag blurred the eulogies to a woman he hardly felt he knew. But the hymns were inescapable and entered directly into his heart as they had done in his childhood. And afterward the reception for old friends was held in the chapel where he had attended Sunday school in the 1930s, now with its newly completed memorial stained-glass window picturing the young Christ teaching the elders, after the painting Mother had done, with twelve-year-old Henry cast forever in the role of the Savior, his hair gleaming.

"What a pity," they all said, "that she couldn't have lived to see it."

What irritated him most, he complained to Margo afterward at the Ramada, was Joey's extended campaign of energetic and pious loving reverence to mother's memory—the taped funeral service for Henry to take home, the staging of this afternoon's event. "The son of a bitch couldn't even stand to walk across his own backyard to go see her. Not that I blame him! Now he wants me to go with him to spread the ashes. The hell with him."

Margo helped him off with his clothes and put him to bed.

Two years later the ashes were still at the funeral home and Joey was still sending thoughtful birthday presents that Henry refused to open for days.

"You wear me out," Margo said. "Why do you have to go on rejecting him? What has he ever done to hurt you?"

# 13

———◦—◦———

Margo and Henry were standing alone at Gate 18 in San Francisco International Airport. Their fellow passengers had hurried off, followed by the flight attendants hauling their bags on little trolleys. Marty was nowhere to be seen.

"Damn!" Margo said it with vehemence. Not simply because she was annoyed but because it was necessary to demonstrate to Henry that she was annoyed. Marty had made a special point of promising to be there on time and she had believed him as she had been believing him all his life. Henry had not believed from long experience and Margo knew this from long experience.

"Why don't we just go ahead to the baggage area? He'll find us there." It was three o'clock. They were in San Francisco for a convention of state legislators. Henry had until five to get to the Sir Francis Drake Hotel to set up his display.

This was Margo's first trip to San Francisco. She hoped it wouldn't be spoiled. She hadn't seen Marty since his twenty-fifth birthday four years ago. Henry was standing, doing nothing, being patient. Margo couldn't bear this.

"Okay," she said. "Let's go get the bags."

Fifteen minutes later there was no Marty. They stood by the

carousel, now stilled, surrounded by their baggage and three bright blue plastic cylinders, each the size of a golf bag, which contained Henry's display.

"Should we consider a cab?" Henry said. "They close down the exposition area at five-thirty and it takes me at least half an hour to set up." He had explained this twice before. He had made it clear all along that he would prefer a cab, but Marty had been extending himself to be cordial for the first time ever.

"You know we can't."

"He can catch up with us."

"He may not know where we'll be."

"Margo." Henry gazed at her steadily. "Tell me that's not true. You didn't tell him? In writing?"

Suddenly the air was full of Marty, who had materialized like a genie.

"Hey, lovebirds!" he sang out, embracing his mother, shaking hands with Henry, grabbing an enormous load of luggage all in one smooth motion as though he were returning a tough ball from the far corner of the court.

Still the professional tennis person. After his years of runthood he had continued doggedly to grow into his nineteenth year, as though he had willed it, to a height of five-feet-ten (that he called five-feet-eleven).

He strode ahead of them through automatic doors to a loading area where his Volkswagen was illegally parked. He pushed himself with his toes inside his running shoes when he walked, making each stride a little surge forward as though he were wading a stream. His arms and torso and neck were thick from weight lifting. He was as tan and vibrant as a native Californian. He was wearing jeans and a tight T-shirt colored fuchsia—almost shocking pink.

Henry stepped around to the front of the Beetle to open the

trunk, but the bumper had been bashed so the lid wouldn't clear it. He straightened up and shot Marty a look.

"Hey, no problem!" said Marty. "You wouldn't believe how much I can stick in the back." He opened a door and began carefully lifting in one piece at a time, turning them this way and that to get maximum use of space. The three blue plastic cylinders still stood on the curb.

A skycap was watching incredulously, to Marty's amusement. "You gonna have room for the engine?" said the skycap.

"Now you, Momma." Marty indicated a space in the back appropriate for a three-year-old child or a miniature poodle. Two skycaps were now watching.

"We've still got to get these cases in," said Henry pointing to the blue objects.

"Sure." Marty placed two of them over Margo's lap. They extended across the luggage, too, almost the full width of the Beetle. Marty had left just enough room for them. Margo sedulously avoided meeting Henry's eye across the top of her burden.

"Okay, Henry, you get in and I'll hand you your blue tube here." Marty ran around to the driver's door and leaped into the seat. "Where to?" He was talking to Henry but looking back at Margo. "You okay there?"

"Sure," she said. "If we crash I'll be armored on all sides."

"The Sir Francis Drake," said Henry. Margo sensed an anxious tension at the top of his head, which was all she could see of him. It was almost four o'clock.

"Hey, no prob!" sang Marty. "It's up on top of Nob Hill."

*If he says that again I'll clobber him,* Margo thought. This was a different Marty, manic, on stage, burning bright. He hustled the Volkswagen through the airport snarl and northward onto the freeway, talking the whole time, pointing out a vista of the Bay that Margo could barely see over the luggage. San Francisco began to take shape out the top two inches of the windshield. Marty's monologue was taking jagged turns. He told Henry that some guy had backed into the VW in the parking lot and messed up the bumper and that he'd tried to borrow another car to come get them. "Did you see those skycaps watching me? They never thought I'd get all this stuff in." That sounded more like the Marty Margo knew and loved—the old Marty who had been holding the world at bay all his life—cocky, making commitments he had no way of meeting, boasting, borrowing, breaking toys and promises. Marty had been the one who could never ask for help, trapped in his bell jar.

When Sandra and Thomas had been bad, Margo wanted to kill them because they were good kids. When Marty had been bad it had made her cry inside.

"Oops," said Marty up front. He'd missed the exit onto Highway 80. Now they would have to do it the hard way. The VW careened into the far right lane to catch the next ramp.

Margo peered out the crack left open to her. They were finally somewhere in the city, climbing hills. She could see the bottom half of first-story windows and the doors and not much else. It seemed to Margo that the car's breathing was becoming labored. She made a mild comment to that effect.

"The hills are what make San Francisco beautiful," Marty said.

"I'm sure that's true, but it doesn't answer my question. What I asked was whether your car has ever done this before."

"When there's an earthquake," said Henry, "do the buildings on top of the hill fall down on the buildings at the bottom of the hill?"

Marty flicked him a grin. "They say real Californians love the earthquakes because they drive the foreigners out."

"Like you?" Henry said.

"They also say VW Beetles can climb walls."

*At least we're all cheerful about it,* Margo thought. She remembered the year that Henry and Marty lived in the same house without speaking to each other, Marty's last dropout year when there was energy for tennis but not for help on the farm. Marty would promise but defer delivery until Henry got so angry he simply ceased to acknowledge Marty's existence.

"Oh hell," said Marty. A green light ahead had turned yellow. Margo could see it through the window because the Volkswagen's angle of approach was approximately forty-five degrees. "Go through! Go through!" Marty was yelling to the car ahead of them, but it stopped, so Marty had to stop, too, like a one-armed trapeze artist, hanging. Instead of using the brake he rode the clutch. Margo had been severely lectured by Henry for doing this in the TR6. She could smell smoke now, presumably from the clutch but conceivably from the top of Henry's head. Henry was saying nothing. Henry was conspicuously quiet.

Three eons later the light changed to green. The Volkswagen shuddered, clawed its way onto the cross street and flung itself up the grade on the far side. It seemed to Margo that this achievement was attained by the force of her will alone.

At two more intersections the lights were green. At a third Marty simply went through the red light. "They'd never stop you for that. It's an unwritten code."

"Life and death," Henry said. "As in North Dakota where it's illegal to pass a stranded motorist in winter."

"Exactly."

They had reached the summit of Nob Hill. The Volkswagen was not boiling because it had no water, Henry announced to no one special. The buildings—as much as Margo could see of them—were large and elegant, permanent-looking, continental. The VW slowed before magnificent gates.

"This is not the Sir Francis Drake," said Henry. "It's the Mark Hopkins."

The Volkswagen responded as though to Henry's words, raced around a corner, encountered a one-way street, backed, tried again, turned, slowed before another hotel.

"This one is the Fairmont," said Henry.

"I know it's right here somewhere."

The Volkswagen scurried three more blocks. The buildings were beginning to look familiar. They had been around twice now.

"Shouldn't we maybe ask?" said Henry mildly.

"I know it's right here somewhere."

"Go ask," said Margo. "This minute."

"Momma! There's nobody to ask."

"Drive in there. Right now."

"That's the Mark Hopkins."

"Do it. Right now. Ask."

The Volkswagen slunk into the courtyard of the Mark Hopkins like a mole at Heaven's gate, halted, breathing deeply beside a Continental whose dark green lacquer was so deep that Margo could see her face in it even from the shadows of her burrow.

The VW door opened. Marty trotted into the hotel foyer, re-emerged, reentered the VW. "It's down on Powell. We'll be there in five minutes."

"Do me a favor," said Henry. "Don't coast down the hill."

By the time they found the Sir Francis Drake Henry had fifteen minutes left to set up his display. They'd gotten lost twice more, having been directed to the Westin Saint Francis, also on Powell but closer to Market. Marty and Henry raced up to the mezzanine with the blue tubes, leaving Margo at the hotel door guarding the Volkswagen.

"Are you afraid someone will steal it?" asked the doorman. Margo couldn't tell whether he was leering at the car or at her. Its engine was still running.

"I'm afraid the trashmen will pick it up. It's got all my favorite shoes in it."

A porter arrived. He and Margo exhumed the bags. "Would you like the car parked, ma'am?" Margo smiled gratefully and accepted the claim check.

There was a clang from the street—a cable car heading upward, jammed with passengers, people clinging to its sides. People having fun. San Francisco. Somehow the sight made the air smell better, like the sea a little.

Margo registered at the desk for herself and Henry, supervised the transportation of bags and Henry's boxes to their suite, an old-fashioned one with a bathtub, a window that opened, a cramped bedroom with the tall, milk-carton feel of old city hotels.

As she gave the porter two dollars she realized what an extraordinarily handsome and gentle boy he was. The semaphore *gay* flashed briefly in a corner of her mind. Certainly that bitchy doorman had been.

Margo had struggled not to be boorish about homosexuality. She had friends at home in Fauquier County who were lesbians. Everyone knew it; no one discussed it. Yet she couldn't help being jolted, when once on a trip with Henry they'd seen men walking the streets holding hands in SoHo. Or even worse, that therapy group she'd bartended for where pairs of men and women were dancing with conspicuous abandon.

"Why does it bother you?" Henry said when she told him about it.

"Why did you get angry when they started using the new liturgy?"

"Because the 1927 service was beautiful and the new one is ugly. Is that what you're trying to say about homosexuality?"

Well, yes, as a matter of fact, that was exactly what she meant. Intellectually she could detach herself from it, but it still made her flesh crawl.

"What was so bad about it?" Henry asked her. "Were they doing something explicit?"

"No—no. I don't know. I guess it wasn't so awful, except to me. Something buried in my past, I suppose. I'm just happy I don't have to face it with Thomas and Marty."

"What would you do if one of them came home and told you he was gay?" Henry asked her. But she couldn't even think about it.

It was the one thing that unsettled her about coming to San Francisco. Well, perhaps one of several—the gays, the drugs, the terrible rate of the AIDS epidemic. She wished Marty would pick some other place to live.

There was a tremendous knocking at the door—Marty excited, Henry remote, as usual.

"We looked everywhere!" Marty exploded. "Where's Henry's stuff? Where's my car? What did you do with them?"

Henry's stuff was two boxes of publications to go in the display booth. "It's okay," he said. "I can take them down in the morning."

"I had the valet service park your car," Margo said, producing the ticket.

"You what! Do you know what that's going to cost? Fifteen dollars!"

"Well, I couldn't just leave it there."

"You could! You could! I leave it everywhere."

"Hoping it'll get stolen?"

"Here," Henry said. "Give me the ticket. I'll get it out for you." His face was telling Margo something she couldn't understand beyond the fact that he hated to have them yelling at each other. To her it had felt like home again.

"Wait," said Marty, mollified now. "Let's eat first." His breeziness was gone, though. He was a little depressed if anything.

Dinner seemed to revive him. They ate in the little hotel restaurant and talked about what his brother and sisters had been up to. Libby was a highly paid flight attendant. Sandra was in New York. Thomas was training in Air Force jets.

Marty was a bit vague about himself. He still made a few bucks from tennis. He worked in a sporting goods store sometimes. He shared an apartment in Larkspur. He'd like to invite them there, he said, but there was nothing to see, no room to stay. Margo felt compelled to worry about his poor prospects, but Henry cut her off—Henry, of all people, was fending for him.

They made plans for the weekend. Henry would rent a car and they would all drive out to the wine country. Tomorrow Marty would be tied up, but he grabbed a handful of brochures from the lobby and shoved them at Margo with recommendations for her day—the cable cars, Fisherman's Wharf, the Maritime Museum.

By 9:30 Margo and Henry were back in their room. Henry was tired. It was 12:30 East Coast time. But Margo needed to talk. Marty wasn't right. "I'm scared for him in this awful city, Henry. He was so strange today. Do you think he was on something?"

"I think you should stop."

"Why?"

"Well, I need the sleep for one thing. Tomorrow's just another workday for me."

"But I'm worried about him. He needs to have a fire built under him. He's got to get going pretty soon, Henry. He's twenty-nine."

Henry sighed, turned his head away from her on the pillow. "What he needs from us is acceptance, not fire. It seems pretty clear that the reason he panicked when you put his car away is that he didn't have the fifteen dollars to get it out. The car isn't even registered properly. I think what we need to do is be supportive. Now please settle down. We can talk about it in the morning." He reached and turned out the light above his head.

Reluctantly Margo lay back, eyes wide open, watching the changing pattern of lights on the ceiling. Outside the window a cable car rumbled by, clanging faintly, the sound diminishing.

What was so scary was that Marty seemed doomed. Had always seemed so. When they were together she could hide it from herself in the bustle of a day's living, but coming back to him like this it was so strong it almost knocked her down, like a bad body smell. It was as though he was being beaten, standing his ground, refusing to flinch, refusing to defend himself. Margo could see the same little boy in him she had always seen.

"Goddam it," Henry said. "I'm exhausted and I can't sleep."

"Why don't you go take a hot bath?"

Henry hated baths. Baths depressed him. Margo made him lie on his stomach and kneaded the muscles in his neck and shoulders until he drifted off.

When she lay back she couldn't relax. Her mind was still on Marty's adolescent years. Now ten years later she saw what she had never admitted to herself—that Marty had never had girlfriends. There were girls in gangs, Sandra's friends mostly.

She tried to remember what Marty had said about his roommate in Larkspur. She couldn't remember whether it was a man or woman.

Marty surprised her the next day by coming back to take her around San Francisco himself. He'd borrowed a better car and took her to Fisherman's Wharf to wander through the shops. She bought shirts for Sandra's kids, a turquoise bracelet for Libby. She wanted to get a blazer for Marty but he didn't like it. He'd always been hard to please about clothes. They went into a place where a computer printed out a picture of them as they sat in front of a video camera—mother and son, cheek-to-cheek, smiling, handsome, both with lovely teeth. Marty liked the printouts so much that he bought four—gave three to Margo and kept one for himself. He took her to lunch in the Carnelian Room on the fifty-second floor of the Bank of America building—spectacular views of San Francisco in every direction, pale stone slender shapes gleaming in the September sunshine now that the morning fog had burned off. One of the buildings was a delicate pyramid, almost an obelisk. Beyond it the bay was cobalt blue across to Oakland. Margo thought the Bay Bridge was the Golden Gate and had to be turned around.

Lunch was Marty's treat. He had money now. If anything this worried Margo more than his being broke. She began to mother him, knowing he would withdraw, unable to restrain herself.

"What are you doing way out here?"

"Surviving. Mom—don't. Be my girlfriend for today."

"I can't help worrying about you. You're my firstborn child and I'm three thousand miles away from you. I can't picture where you live or what you're doing. Half the time you haven't even had a phone."

"How would you and Henry like to ride up to Tiburon for dinner tonight? There's a place we can sit, right out in the middle of a marina with all the boats around us, right on the water."

"That sounds nice. And I'm watching you change the subject."

"Or we could ride the ferry to Sausalito. It goes right by Alcatraz."

"We were so close when you were little. Do you remember those things we learned to sing together—from *Man of La Mancha* and *Jesus Christ Superstar?* You had a wonderful ear for music. You loved the Beach Boys."

"Did you know that the Indians tried to reclaim Alcatraz after it was closed as a prison? They went out in boats and established a beachhead."

Margo started to hum a few bars of "Barbara Ann" and was frozen into silence by Marty's glare. "I wasn't singing loud," she said.

"Momma—I won't be mothered. You can just stop. I'm trying to do everything I can to make this a pleasant visit for you." They both had ordered abalone and salad, but Marty wasn't eating.

"San Francisco scares me," Margo said.

"Why, for Heaven's sake?"

"All this business about gays and AIDS. I just can't help worrying. I mean I know you're not gay or anything but the whole idea of it just scares me so, and—" She stopped. He was staring at her with an expression she couldn't read and that scared her even more. "What?" she said.

"You just won't quit, will you."

She wanted to hug him. She wanted to run.

He put his hand on her wrist. "Here," he said. "Let me give you something to think about. I've been saving my money. I think I can start classes at San Francisco State this month. Part-time anyhow. With the credits I had at Blacksburg I should be able to get a degree in about three semesters, once I get going."

She had to believe it. She had heard it a dozen times before and every time she believed it because there was no other choice. She took his hand and squeezed it without saying anything. She was trying not to cry. Marty was still talking about school, but it wasn't quite definite yet, as it had always been not quite definite, but he was running ahead now, to an M.B.A. or maybe even law school. He had even begun to pick at his lunch.

Margo gazed out at the city below them. She'd almost forgotten it was there. Everything seemed to float in a haze of warm sunlight. "What would you think of coming back to Tech to finish up? You could keep your money. There's still a little of your daddy's trust to help you. It can't be used for anything else."

Marty was slowly shaking his head, smiling, ruefully, shaking his head.

"Why not? There'd still be a hundred and fifty miles between us if you need privacy."

By Sunday afternoon Margo and Henry were on their way down the coast along California Route 1. In the distance was the Pacific gleaming like an eye. Close in were endless fields of brussels sprouts.

"I can't believe it," Henry was saying. "All this fantastic coastline and they grow brussels sprouts right down to the water."

Saturday in the Napa Valley had been a qualified success. The suburban sprawl north of the Golden Gate had depressed Margo, but once beyond Novato the countryside opened up. Some of the trees were strange-looking but at least there were green leaves and fields to ease the eye after three days of stone and pavement.

She had loved the wineries with their polished Victorian interiors and cool catacombs. Especially she loved tasting all the wines. She became enamored of a gamay rouge made by one very small house and had two cases shipped home for presents.

Ultimately Henry and Marty had wearied of the tours and sat in the parking lot talking while Margo made the final tour by herself. When she came back a little silly from all the sampling they were both asleep in the car.

On the way back she had sensed a peace between the two of them that had never existed in the years she had been fostering it at home. It made the whole California trip worthwhile to her.

"What did you and Marty talk about while I was gone yesterday?" she said without looking at Henry. She had a feeling that he'd been waiting for the question.

"He asked me not to talk about it—at least parts of it."

Margo closed her eyes. Her heart was closing her throat, so that it was difficult for her to speak. "I don't suppose you could break such a confidence."

"He was upset with you. He needed to ventilate with me rather than—" He stopped. Margo was crying. "Oh, for Heaven's sake. It wasn't that bad. I'll tell you at least the gist of it. He was angry that you thought he might be gay. Apparently that's come up before, at least by inference. He felt you were manipulating him, trying to pull him back into the nest. That thing about singing in the restaurant, whatever it was, really got to him."

Margo still had her eyes closed. "You're saying he's not—" She couldn't make herself use the word *gay*.

"Margo, you're missing the point. He said it wasn't an issue. It seemed clear to me that he didn't want to deal with it where we're concerned and I didn't push it. If I had, the conversation would have ended. He said he'd gotten off cocaine. My guess is he's still having problems with it. I asked what either of us could do and he said just be there. He said he loved you but you drive him crazy, and I told him my mother did the same thing to me."

"Oh boy," Margo said. "That's just great. I can just see the two of you chortling about manipulative mothers. To think that's what you got together about after all these years when I've been trying so hard to please everybody, playing Cupid, playing mediator, playing kiss-my-fanny, playing hooker! Oh boy, oh boy! Goddamn you, Henry. You make me sick!"

"Margo, will you listen. Will you let me finish!"

"I don't want to hear any more. I'm sorry I asked. You know, when a child is little you have a wonderful time with him. You know who he is and he knows who you are, and you love each other in the purest possible way. There is a web of love between your two hearts. Then he becomes a teenager and he loses his essence and turns into a walking snake pit. For years this goes on, and you scream at each other and hate each other, and all the time a mother goes on hoping and waiting for that real person to come back to her in a mature form. That's all I wanted. I just wanted my son back. Instead you joined forces with him."

Henry said nothing. He continued to drive steadily, evenly, just as he always did. Once he had told her his father had taught him to drive as though there were eggs in the back seat. He ran his life as though there were eggs in the back seat. It made Margo want to scream.

She turned her back to him and tried to sleep. If she let him he would say nothing until they got to wherever it was they were going. Then he would ask her if she were hungry as though nothing had happened.

Henry cleared his throat as though it were filled with glue. "I have to say this, Margo," he said finally. "I feel sorry for Marty. He told me he finally realizes that he's been trying to run away from himself, and that's the only thing he's accomplished in three years."

"He said he was going back to school. He's been saving money." Margo turned her head a little toward Henry without sitting up. "Was he just saying that to make me shut up?"

For a long time he said nothing. When he spoke he had to clear his throat twice. "He's almost thirty. He's feeling very old. And he does understand you and it makes him want to cry, just as it does me. You've tried so hard to make everybody love one another, and all we felt was used. That's the saddest part. All you wanted was just to have us be loving. And all we did was clench our teeth."

Margo was crying.

"I'm sorry, honey. Sometimes we just have to wait for them to crash. Sometimes it seems as though there's no way one human can touch another human."

"You could hold me," she said.

"Would that help?" He seemed surprised.

"It might."

Henry stopped the car on a wide place on the shoulder. Then he gathered her carefully in his arms and stroked her face.

"I was thinking," he said after a minute, "how good you were to me in the intensive care unit."

"That was nine years ago."

"I can't remember whether I ever thanked you."

. . .

They stopped at an upscale hotel in Santa Cruz, above the water and adjacent to the municipal pier stretching half a mile into the bay. Even at off-season rates it was high, but Henry came back to say he'd signed in anyhow. He led Margo to a waterfront room with a balcony, dumped the bags, threw open the sliding glass doors to let in sea air and sounds.

Margo began to unpack a few things, then lay down exhausted. The last thing she remembered was Henry trying the TV for news.

When she woke he was asleep beside her, close enough that their shoulders touched but face down, his arms wrapped around a pillow.

She tried to remember the phrase he'd used about Marty's being gay—that it didn't matter. That it wasn't important. Something like that. What was that supposed to mean? Yes? No? It meant, Mother, keep out. Don't come to my apartment. Don't ask questions.

She turned her head and looked out through the glass doors Henry had left open. She could see sky and part of a land mass. Somehow the sun was setting in the wrong direction. It was after five.

Shivering, she got up and slid the door closed, then stopped to watch three gulls at the water's edge struggling nastily over something rotten-looking. On the far side of the pier a few boats were moored. She could see traffic going out onto the pier toward a cluster of shops of some kind.

"Hello." Henry was looking at her. She came to sit beside him.

"I can't stand not knowing things. I can't live with uncertainty."

"About what?"

"About Marty. My God, is my son into drugs? Could he have AIDS? What did you say about the sex thing?" She got up to look for her purse, found it, couldn't remember why she wanted it.

"I told you he said it wasn't an issue."

"But what does that mean? Is he or isn't he?"

Henry sat up, fished sneakers out of his bag and put them on. "Let's walk," he said. "Let's go out on that pier. There are restaurants out there."

Margo sat on the edge of the bed with her hands on her lap, her eyes closed.

"Come on, honey. Get your sneakers."

She couldn't make herself move. "This is very hard, Henry. What do I say when we meet him Monday?"

He put out a hand and pulled her up. Hugged her long enough to steady her.

They walked slowly out on the pier, boulevard-wide, twenty feet above water that was avocado green when Margo looked down into it. The swells were more like a lake than ocean, she thought. Below them a boy was experimenting with a wind-surfer, falling and falling again, just as he seemed to get under way.

They peered into the windows of the restaurants and souvenir shops. Margo inspected unfamiliar-looking fish at an open stall. Out that far the wind blew steadily. Even with a sweater she was cold.

Beyond the shops they found a corner in the lee of some undefinable structures, away from the cars and people. The sun was dropping toward the horizon. A zipper of gold extended along the water toward them.

"The point is, he's got to be left on his own," Henry said quietly. He raised his head. "I heard a seal bark."

"Where?"

"Listen—more than one. Two. Several."

He grabbed Margo's hand and they hurried toward the sound, farther out on the pier to a railed hatch, open so they could look below and see the trestlework and down into the water sloshing against the pilings. The lowest beams each looked almost as wide as a lunch counter and formed a series of catwalks lengthwise and crosswise about four feet above the water level. And sprawled about on those beams like throw pillows Margo saw what must have been a dozen California sea lions basking and shining in the last rays of sunlight—quizzical, whiskery, comic, massive. The largest was as big as a fourteen-hand pony. He waved his snout and barked his bathtub chorus. Three others joined him, the sound racketing up like pebbles against tin. Margo realized there were more seals swimming around—there must have been twenty or thirty altogether.

They reminded her of an Italian wedding reception. The huge one directly under them would be the grandmother, the two moth-eaten ones were the father and godfather, surrounded by aunts, uncles, cousins, musicians. And showing off their beauty in the water below were the swains and the lasses, ogling, nudging, Indian wrestling.

Suddenly there was a raucous chorus of rubbery whooping, as though the bride had thrown her bouquet.

Margo sensed that Henry was watching her. She was grinning in spite of the dull ache inside.

# 14

———— •◆• ————

Margo had periods of despair. She blamed them on her chemistry, her age.

The symptoms were feelings of failure as a mother, of inadequacy as a wife. She had lost touch with all the truths that once seemed so conveniently at hand.

"My children defeat me. My life defeats me," she told Henry.

"It's the first inkling of your sainthood. Your soul is cleansing itself."

On a Saturday morning in August Margo and Libby sat in the kitchen talking about Sandra. Libby had made breaking away from home a long and leisurely procedure with few wounds and minimal corrective surgery. This week she was home after six weeks in Chicago. At twenty-one she made a startling salary with United Airlines.

She had sliced a half banana into a cut-glass bowl containing discrete layers of Grape Nuts, Wheat Chex, and Rice Krispies.

This month she was drinking herb tea. Being beautiful was her stock-in-trade.

Margo was having half a bagel and black coffee, losing back the five pounds she had gained and lost twice this year. New acquaintances often assumed she was Libby's real mother because of the dark hair and the cheekbones. Henry was outside with the tractor as he had been since six. He never slept late, even on Saturdays, and had long ago had coffee. Henry was less upset with Sandra than the rest of the family, although more than anyone he had hated her screaming at Margo.

Sandra had returned to Broad Run without Ed and had been living for two months with her three small children in a ramshackle barn-apartment out the Falls Road, leaving the kids with whoever would take them, working as a waitress, staying out all night with a miscellany of waiters, lawyers, ambulance drivers.

Libby was scandalized. "It's not right for a twenty-seven-year-old woman. She's like the worst of our flight attendants. She's gotten totally irresponsible. Look how she's dressing. I'm beginning to wonder if it really was all Ed's fault."

"Oh, Libby," said Margo sadly. She poured coffee for herself at the stove. As always, where Sandra was concerned, Margo was torn between rage and pity. To have seamless Libby standing upon virtue only underscored Sandra's helplessness. Yet Sandra had no business being helpless. It was a luxury not permitted to mothers of three. Despite all Margo's trauma about becoming a grandmother, she now worried compulsively about the kids.

"They're growing up without learning anything," she said. "She's so frantic, she forgets they're there. She dumps food on the table, then goes and talks on the telephone. She doesn't even eat with them. Eric has the table manners of a duck."

"A duck?" Libby looked at her in amusement.

"Yes, a duck. He hardly even uses his hands."

"I like that," Libby said. "A duck."

Henry clumped through in his work shoes, fished out a can of Port Clyde sardines, opened it, drained the extra oil into the cat dish by his feet. With a salad fork he carefully removed the sardines from the can and inserted them into pita bread pockets. Then he poured a glass of apple juice and sat down.

Margo and Libby watched this ritual in silence as they had many times before.

"That makes me nauseous," Libby said thoughtfully.

"Wrong," said Henry. "I am nauseous. You are nauseated. That's a paraphrase of a famous quote: 'No, madam. I do not smell. It is you who smells. I stink.'"

Henry ate Port Clyde sardines because they were lower than eggs in cholesterol and he was more or less on the Pritikin diet. He had once mentioned driving out to Stonington on the tip of Deer Isle, Maine, and having lobster stew in a six-booth restaurant with someone he'd loved before Margo. The restaurant overlooked the Port Clyde cannery.

"What are we going to do about the children?" Margo said scowling at him.

"Who's we?" Henry knew which children. "Why can't they go to Muriel?"

Margo ignored this. Muriel was currently luxuriating in Miami Beach. "Sandra couldn't wait to have them bing bing bing. Now she's abandoned them."

"Every time I see them, she has them lined up behind her like a mother duck," Henry said.

Libby looked at her mother and giggled. Margo closed her eyes to eliminate Henry for a moment. There was the whole downstairs where they could stay, practically an apartment. The question was who could stand how much of what. Libby would pitch in because Libby always pitched in, but you never knew when she was going to run off to Istanbul. The kids would drive Henry crazy. This was a given. Margo set it aside like an egg yolk for later.

The real question was Sandra, who had shown no inclination to stay any longer than it took to drop the kids off for free protective custody.

No, the real question was the kids, who were clearly feeling superfluous. The one person who could always be counted on to love them was Margo. After her initial shock at becoming a grandmother had worn off with the passage of time and Christmas visits home, the children began to take on human form, melting Margo's resistance and, more significantly, increasing her concern that these small people were not getting a decent start in life. As with all Sandra-Margo discussions these dialogues tended to be more acrimonious than substantive, so that Sandra came home with a chip on her shoulder or pouted in New York.

Margo's one visit to the apartment on Riverside Drive had been difficult. She came away convinced that the children were on an emotional starvation diet that left them lonely on the one hand and undisciplined on the other.

"I felt so helpless," she told Henry. "There was almost nothing I could do to rescue them."

"Almost?"

"You should see them, Henry. Eric is a sweet, serious little old man. Jennifer is the wild woman with her temper and all that gold hair. Very bright. You can see Sandra in her. And Hadley is the cherub—"

"Almost?"

Margo looked at him. "Was I babbling?"

"You said there was *almost* nothing you could do. . . ."

"Oh well, that. Yes. I did take them to the zoo one day without announcing it to the whole world."

"Did you know Sandra called me at the office that day?"

"She did?"

"She thought you'd kidnapped them."

"What did you say?"

"I promised to ship them back by UPS if you brought them home to Virginia."

Margo picked up her cup, rinsed it, and put it in the dishwasher. "The real question," she said, "is which will be worse—Sandra's mouth or those dirty looks of yours."

It was quarter of two in the morning when Sandra came in—to pick up the kids, she said. She'd left them with Margo because she couldn't get a sitter while she worked Saturday night.

When Margo suggested it would be easier to let them sleep, Sandra didn't put up much of an argument. She dropped wearily into Henry's TV chair, lighted a cigarette, left it sitting in the ashtray.

"Can we just be friends?" she said. She was dressed in a black miniskirt, a long-sleeved white nylon blouse with flared cuffs, a black bow tie. She removed the tie and unbuttoned the collar. She didn't look like Margo, but she had a lot of her features—the straight nose, the intense eyes. Margo was softer. Sandra was stronger, wilder, more like a seagull, less like a duck. It was Margo who was the duck. A decent lady mallard.

"What's wrong?" she said.

"Well—I'm not pregnant. I don't seem to have any AIDS symptoms. That's a start."

"So—what's wrong?"

"Mother!" Sandra put her hands out in front of her as though she were holding a melon between them, then dropped her hands into her lap. "Does something have to be wrong for me to want to be friends?"

"No."

"Thank you." Sandra stretched out, raised her feet to the coffee table without removing her shoes. Then she changed her mind, rose, went to the cabinet, took out the vodka, and made herself a drink.

Margo watched the performance. "But aside from that," she said, "what's wrong?"

Tears ran down Sandra's cheeks. "Everything," she said. "I don't have anything left in life."

"Except Eric and Jennifer and Hadley."

"Oh, Mom. They're work. They're my prison. I love them. You know I love them. But that isn't what I need."

"No going back to Ed?"

"I'm sure that as soon as his current blonde dumps him he'll be back begging."

"Oh." This was the first time Sandra had said what was wrong between her and Ed, who had doted on her and the children as far as Margo could determine. If he was having affairs it wasn't a thing Margo could deal with. "He *tells* you about them?"

"Only when they abuse him. Then he wants comfort."

"That's disgusting."

"Tell me about it. And now I've gotten even by being as disgusting as I could. Wasn't that smart of me? Mom, is there a single decent man anywhere on this planet?"

Margo didn't answer for a long while, watching the smoke rise from Sandra's untouched cigarette in the ashtray. This was the second cigarette, perhaps the third. She'd been taking one drag, then setting down each of them and forgetting it was there. Margo sighed. "Oh, honey," she said sadly. "When you were little I knew all the answers. Now I don't know anything anymore. Would you like to come here and stay with the kids? We could make you a separate apartment with all that space downstairs. I don't know what to offer. I'm just so worried about the children."

Sandra said nothing. Put her head back and closed her eyes. Sat up again and pulled her shoes off one at a time, letting them fall where gravity took them, just as she had done all her life. She leaned back and closed her eyes again.

Watching her, waiting, Margo began to dream of having the children with her as Sandra went off to work daytimes to a reputable certified public accounting firm. Margo would get three ponies, just as she'd had for her own children, and start the grandchildren riding before fall. (Eric was plenty big enough already.) And a fourth pony that would be white with a full set of black harness and a red wagon for it to pull. She could start looking next Saturday at the Marshall auction. She wouldn't say anything to the children yet, but she could picture herself taking them out to see the first pony when she brought it home.

One Saturday morning Margo laid her crop on top of the refrigerator. It slipped off and fell down behind. When Henry helped her move the refrigerator out from the wall they found a yellowed sheet of drawing paper. "Look at this," she said, smoothing the edges.

It was a formal pact Thomas and Libby had drawn up "in honor of Margo Calef and Henry Calef." Undated, handwritten in Thomas' version of Gothic script, it bore a rococo design at the

the top with his and Libby's names worked into the filigree, and lacy spandrel decorations in all four corners. This was the text:

This is a peace treaty
We will try our hardest not to fight these
rules will help us:
1. No violent physical contact
2. There will be no tattleing
3. No parenting over each other
4. There will be no anger shed through our mouths
5. We will be kind to each other and share
Signitures
*Elizabeth Calef*              *Thomas Anthony Bishop*
Please help us
GOD

"I don't recall any outbreak of peace," Henry said. "Do you?"

"I think it lasted a week. But they tried."

"We all tried."

"Maybe trying is all there is."

Henry considered this for a few moments. "Maybe you're right. In my family it all had to do with ancestors and continuity. You were glued together whether or not you tried. Things were important because they represented continuity, and that was how you knew what you were. That's why my mother got so upset at Libby's having the banjo clock, because the bloodline was broken."

Margo had been polishing silver at the sink. She stopped and gazed at Henry. "No wonder you have trouble hugging people."

This was in late September. For more than a month Sandra had lived in the basement area with Eric and Jennifer and Hadley, who all seemed to be upstairs more than down.

"It's your fault," Henry told Margo. "If you discouraged them they wouldn't be up here climbing on me all the time."

Margo smiled at him. "You're an attractive nuisance."

"That's true. That's how I got you. It's my real identity. If I have some continuity to pass along, that's what it'll be."

That afternoon Henry had to drive to Front Royal to meet a lawyer, and took Eric along for company because Eric loved riding in the Triumph. Eric was still only six and had trouble seeing much if he was locked into the seat belt, but he liked having the top down and feeling the sun and wind on his face, and he could see the trees and the rising of the Blue Ridge skyline if not the road ahead.

After Henry's business with the lawyer they stopped for Big Macs, then headed down the Interstate toward home. As the sun dropped toward the ridge and the shadows lengthened, Eric's eyes began to glaze.

Henry heard a sound and realized that Eric was singing, matching the note of the car's exhaust, as the pitch rose and fell with his foot's pressure on the gas pedal.

And suddenly the year was 1931, and seven-year-old Henry Calef was stretched full length across the back seat of his father's 1931 Pontiac, somnolent, humming with the motor's song, loving the feel of coarse mohair against his cheek, loving the dip of the power lines from pole to pole out the window, loving the new car's smell, loving the music of the exhaust pipe, loving his father's foot on the accelerator, loving his father.